For Liz, Mateo, Tomas, and Alessia

CONTENTS

INTRODUCTION

A former industry-leading innovator in the technology sector loses its market dominance in a matter of months and now struggles to survive. The chief executive officer (CEO) of a large retailer is forced to resign after having an inappropriate relationship with a coworker. The founder and chair of the board of the same company is pushed out after it's revealed that he knew about the relationship and did nothing to inform the board. It seems that stories of corruption and scandal are now so commonplace that we don't even react anymore. Our sense of trust and confidence in senior leaders has been eroded. Survey after survey finds employee engagement is chronically, cripplingly low. Managers say the new generation of workers is unmotivated and feel entitled, while members of Generation Y say they're simply not interested in rising through the ranks in the traditional way. Meanwhile, you and your colleagues feel overworked and pulled in about a dozen different directions at once.

These aren't separate problems. I believe they're all part of one crisis, a crisis that companies worldwide are spending an estimated $60 billion trying to solve—and getting nowhere.

It's a crisis in leadership.

At a moment when our world is more complicated than ever, is changing faster than ever, and is more radically transparent than ever, we desperately need our leaders to be stronger than ever. And they're not. They're failing us. And we're becoming disillusioned.

I've been studying leadership for 25 years. As an employee I've worked for some great leaders and some who were not so great. I know firsthand the effect leadership has on employee engagement and organizational performance. As a consultant, I've worked with thousands of leaders and hundreds of organizations. And I've held leadership roles, and I currently hold an executive position at Knightsbridge Human Capital Solutions. I know at a personal level how challenging leadership can be if you want to do it well on a consistent basis. I also know how great it can be when you get it right.

I talk to leaders every day who know that the world has changed for them. Some feel they are not keeping up. Others believe there is something fundamentally wrong with how we have come to think about leadership. They know their organizations are struggling just to stay abreast of a changing world, and they know that in their desperation they're *settling*. When everything on your to-do list is urgent, things such as inspiration and motivation seem like luxuries. You feel like the leadership parts of your role are just that: parts, something separate that you do from the corner of your desk.

But leadership is not a luxury. You can't settle, or you risk becoming lame. Your organization needs great leaders at all levels, now more than ever. You need to be the best leader you can possibly be. The issue is that leadership has changed, and you are now under more pressure than ever before. Let's look at a few of the big ones:

1. *The Pressure to Differentiate:* Whether it's a private sector company or a public sector organization, every enterprise is trying to differentiate itself. All organizations have competitors, whether for market share or government funding, and now the competition is fierce. Whatever competitive advantage you thought you had seems to have a smaller and smaller shelf life, as rivals copy it almost overnight. You face unrelenting pressure to innovate and look for ways to stand out from the crowd.

2. *The Pressure to Execute Strategy:* You face tremendous pressure to execute strategy. If you've been a leader for a while, you know how hard this can be—success is elusive for many organizations. Research repeatedly shows that only 10 to 30 percent of organizations ever succeed at executing their strategy. Our research at Knightsbridge suggests that part of the reason is that boards and executive teams spend a lot more time talking about what the strategy should be than about how to put it into practice. Many clients have also worked with large strategy consulting firms who do a good job of helping them create strategy but then leave without ever discussing how to get it done. Yet from where I sit it's clear that there's a deep connection between strategy and leadership: Leaders create the strategy, and they need to work together to align the organization. It's their responsibility to ensure that everyone from the front line to the senior team understands the plan. Gaps in leadership will create gaps in execution.

3. *The Pressure to Manage Complexity:* A global study conducted by IBM of 1,500 CEOs found that complexity is a big challenge for leaders today.[1] Eighty percent of leaders surveyed believed the future business environment is going to be even more complex than today's. Less than 50 percent were confident they would have the ability to deal with it. Complexity isn't just increasing, it is also accelerating. As a leader, you will need to help your employees and organization manage this heightened level of complexity in your business environment. You must also do it at a time when you feel like you have diminished power. The days of command and control are over, and now you must influence and bring stakeholders along with you as they try to manage the complexity in their own lives.

4. *The Pressure to Create Enduring Value:* You are also under continuous pressure to deal with ever-increasing expectations from customers, boards, and shareholders. The scrutiny you are under is intense. Customers want value and will go wherever

they must to get it. Their loyalty is fleeting. Boards and shareholders want a short-term increase in share price while creating long-term enterprise value—not an easy tension to manage for senior leaders.

5. *The Pressure to Build Future Talent:* You also cannot focus solely on the present. You are being called upon to build the next generation of leaders. The challenge you face is that after years of shedding costs and people, organizations are now realizing there are significant gaps in their leadership pipelines and succession plans. It seems like everyone finally understands that leadership does matter. The problem is we have a new generation of employees who aren't necessarily that keen on taking leadership roles. We have demographic trends working against us.

If you are like the leaders I work with every day, you personally feel the impact of all these pressures. You feel the increased ambiguity of your business environment. You can feel the scrutiny you are under. You understand the high level of accountability you have for the success of your organization. You are keenly aware of the impact you must drive with customers, employees, and other stakeholders.

Redefining How You Lead

But what you also realize is that when you think of these pressures all together it becomes clear to you that old models of leadership just won't cut it anymore. It's time to redefine leadership for the new world we're living in. What worked in the past isn't going to work in the future. More is expected of leaders today. All of us as leaders need to start demanding more of ourselves.

There is an emerging set of new leadership expectations that is redefining how each of us will need to lead in the future. As a leader you will need to:

- *Align and engage.* You need to understand your company's strategy and your role in executing it. You must then align and engage employees so that they can effectively deploy the strategy in a way that ultimately delivers value to customers, shareholders, and society.

- *Take an enterprise-wide perspective*. You must define your role and success at the company level. This means you will need to collaborate across silos and do what's right for customers and the entire organization. It's a "one company" mind-set that needs to be shared by all leaders in your organization.
- *Build relationships*. In our interconnected and interdependent world, relationships matter more than ever. You have to invest time in getting to know internal and external stakeholders. You must also build relationships with a foundation of trust and transparency.
- *Master uncertainty*. Today's increasingly complicated business environment creates a lot of challenging situations and risk. Your role as a leader is to create focus and help employees deal with ambiguity and the stress it brings.
- *Develop other leaders*. You must leave a legacy of strong leadership within your organization that goes beyond yourself. It's about making your leaders stronger so that they can make your organization stronger.
- *Model the values*. You cannot be focused exclusively on your own personal agenda or team goals. The organization's vision, values, and goals trump ego and self-interest. This means balancing strong self-confidence with humility. You also need to set the bar high for yourself as a leader because mediocrity in leadership isn't acceptable anymore. It never was.

All leaders today are being called upon to redefine how they lead. This process starts with you, and it starts now. Are you ready?

The Leadership Contract

Let's begin with an analogy. You know the feeling you get when you're online, and in order to buy that service or product, you have to click that Agree button? Maybe you're doing your banking, downloading music, or watching a movie—almost anything you do these days requires this button. You know you are agreeing to pages of tiny single-spaced text outlining a set of complicated terms and conditions, but you go ahead and click Agree without really thinking about it.

Only 7 percent of people ever read those terms and conditions.[2] But with that simple click, you are agreeing to quite a lot. You have some sense that you have just agreed to a contract, but you don't know what it entails. You don't understand the fine print.

I believe something similar is happening in leadership today. Lots of leaders have clicked Agree to take on a leadership role without thinking through the terms that come with what I call the *leadership contract.*

You may have clicked Agree for a valid reason—to get the promotion, the higher salary, the perks, the power, or the opportunity to have a real impact—but if you don't fully appreciate what you have signed up for, you won't be effective in leading through the pressures of today's business environment.

Redefining leadership for the future begins with recognizing that there is a leadership contract. It's not a legal or formal contract that you sign. Instead, it is a personal one. It represents the commitment you must personally make to be a great leader. It's a deep commitment to redefine how you lead and become the leader for the future. And when you sign the leadership contract, you are agreeing to a set of terms that you must live up to.

Here they are. Here's the fine print.

1. *Leadership Is a Decision*

Every leader's story begins with a decision. I have heard lots of people describe a moment in their career when they made the conscious decision to be a leader, whether it was their first promotion or the day they stepped into the executive suite. These moments demand that we reflect on why we want to lead, whether we are ready for a new role, and how committed we are to becoming great leaders. This term of the leadership contract demands that you make the personal commitment to be the best leader you can be.

2. Leadership Is an Obligation

Once you decide to lead, you quickly learn you are going to be held to a higher standard. You also realize that you have obligations that go beyond yourself. It's not just about what is best for your career anymore. You have obligations to your customers and employees, your organization, and the communities in which you do business. This term of the leadership contract demands that you step up to your accountabilities and live up to your obligations as a leader.

3. Leadership Is Hard Work

Leadership is hard, and it's getting harder. We have to stop pretending that it is easy or that some quick-fix idea is going to make things better. You need to develop the resilience and determination to tackle the hard work of leadership. You need personal resolve to rise above the daily pressures and lead your organization into the future. This term of the leadership contract demands that you get tough and do the hard work that you must do as a leader.

4. Leadership Is a Community

In our complex world, no one leader will have all the answers. The idea of the lone hero who can save us all was yesterday's model of leadership. Today, we need to build a strong community of leaders. Imagine if you and your colleagues were all fully committed to being great leaders and focused on supporting one another to be better—this would set your organization apart. This term of the leadership contract demands that you connect with others to create a strong community of leaders in your organization—a community where there is deep trust and support, and where you know everyone has your back and where all leaders share the collective aspiration to be great leaders.

A Word of Warning

This book is going to ask a lot of you. It has to because leadership needs to be redefined for the future. Your organization needs you to be the best leader you can be. It needs you to be a great leader.

I will ask you to reflect on your own approach to leadership and what it needs to look like in the future. There will be times when you may feel overwhelmed by the ideas in this book. You may feel they are completely unrealistic. But you'll also realize something you already know—these ideas are ones you've already thought about. Deep down you know that we all must redefine how we are leading today. We all have to. It's not just you. You will also need to think hard about whether you are ready to commit to accepting the four terms of the leadership contract and becoming a great leader, the kind of leader your company needs you to be. You can't be a good or average leader any longer. You can't make leadership only a part of your job, something you focus on only when you have a few minutes of spare time. Instead, you need to make leadership your whole job. It's time to aspire for more. It's time for you to be a great leader. But this is going to take some serious work on your part.

If you're not ready right now, you might want to put this book back on the shelf for a while. But if you believe, as I do, that we desperately need great leadership today, then read on. And if the ideas in this book speak to you, I hope you'll join others who share your passion at www.thecommunityofleaders.com.

CHAPTER 1

My Personal Leadership Story

Great leaders aren't born; they are made—made and shaped by their experiences. Gandhi's mother was very religious and influenced by Jainism, a religion founded on the idea of nonviolence toward all creatures. A village schoolteacher refused to teach a young Susan B. Anthony long division because she was a girl. Margaret Thatcher gained experience weathering criticism when, as education minister in the early 1970s, budget cuts earned her the nickname the "milk snatcher." When Richard Branson was about seven years old, his mother, Eve, left him three miles away from his home on the way back from school so he would be forced to figure out how to get home on his own. She did it to help him overcome his crippling shyness. It took him 10 hours, but he did it and it helped him become the person and the leader he is today.

Like Gandhi, Anthony, Thatcher, and Branson, every leader has a story. But most leaders aren't fully aware of how their experiences have shaped them to be the leaders they are now. I believe it's crucial for leaders to take time to think about their history and their personal leadership story.

Take a moment to think of the key experiences that have shaped you as a leader. I hope some stories are already coming to mind for you. Some will be stories of peak experiences when you had a significant impact, when you were at your best. Others will be more negative—moments when you struggled, when your personal resolve was tested. Reflecting on all of these moments of leadership will give you a clearer vision of who you are as a leader and why you lead the way you do.

I have seen it hundreds of times in my work. In leadership development programs, I like to take people through an exercise that helps them build a Personal Leadership Timeline: a list of the key experiences, both positive and negative, they believe have shaped them as leaders. These stories can come from childhood, school, work, or life in a community. This kind of personal reflection is easier for some people than for others, but everyone I have worked with has come away from this exercise with a renewed sense of enthusiasm and commitment for their leadership roles.

My own leadership story is based on several critical experiences. I'm going to share my story with you because it's important for you to understand where the ideas in this book come from and because I hope it will help you reflect on your own personal leadership story.

Is Leadership Worth Dying For?

Most leaders don't ever have to ask themselves this question. I faced it in my very first full-time job.

Do you remember how you felt when you first started your working life? If you were like me, you wanted to change the world, to really show the value you could bring to an organization. I got a job with a large public sector organization that helped some of the neediest people in society, providing financial support and services to help people get back to school or find a job.

Most of my colleagues were nice people. They were very dedicated to their clients. But they weren't that dedicated to the organization. Most showed up at 8:30 AM and left at 4:30 PM sharp every single day. Maybe they had been turned off by the bland working environment. Everything in the office was beige—the walls, the floors, even the desks and chairs. Even the people seemed beige—or at least bland.

The supervisors and managers were decent individuals, too, but they weren't very inspiring. They did what they were told. They respected the hierarchy and their place in it. Senior management seemed distant. Few employees had direct access to them, and as far as I could tell, they didn't have much impact on the organization.

A month after I started, I was already wondering whether this was really the place for me.

You see, I had done what I was supposed to do. I went to college, got good grades, and landed a solid full-time job. All I had to do now was to be loyal, and the organization would take care of me until I retired. This was to the old-fashioned concept known as job security. But I was realizing it wasn't enough to build a career on. I wanted not just to have an impact on my clients' lives but to make a difference to the organization as a whole. This was the moment I learned how much the culture of an organization can undermine an employee's sense of engagement.

Things improved a little when I started working as a career counselor. This role was better aligned with my own interests in not just giving a handout but in giving a hand up. I started to feel like I was running a new business within a large organization. I soon learned I had a strong entrepreneurial side. I was a builder— not a maintainer.

My work got the attention of a senior manager named Zinta. She was a quiet and reserved person whom I had only known from a distance. She started coming by my office to talk about my work and the new programs I was building. In those discussions, I told her some of my ideas for improving our work environment. One day, she said, "We need someone like you in management. You're a big-picture thinker. You have a strategic mind and know how to get things done. This would really help our management team."

Nobody had ever said anything like that to me before. As a result of that conversation, I began to think about myself differently. I began reading books on management. I wanted to learn more about what Zinta saw in me.

A few weeks later Zinta dropped by my office again. This time she shared with me an idea she had. She suspected that I wanted to have a greater impact on the organization, and I agreed. She then told me she was setting up a committee to find ways to make our work environment more positive. She asked if I would be interested in helping her out, and I jumped at the opportunity.

Much to my surprise, as the work of our committee began to take effect, things actually started to improve. Employees became more enthusiastic. The organization was starting to feel more positive. Everyone was more engaged. You could feel the changes starting to happen in that place. While the walls, floors, and desks were still beige in color, the workplace had more life and vitality. This was the moment I learned that the culture of an organization could be changed for the better, and that one person could make a difference. That person was Zinta.

Things were going pretty well for me. My job was fulfilling. The work environment was more positive and energizing. I was feeling like I was having a real impact. Then disaster struck. Zinta was diagnosed with lung cancer and she had to leave immediately to start treatment.

She was gone for several months. And as soon as she left, the changes we worked so hard to create began to slip away. Upper management disbanded the committe Zinta had started. They told those of us on Zinta's committee to focus on doing our own jobs and to leave the organizational stuff to them. Those of us who worked with Zinta started to be passed up for promotions. I was told I didn't have what it took to be a manager. My engagement eroded even further. I was frustrated, but even more than that, I was confused. I couldn't understand why upper management wouldn't want us to create a better work environment. Plus, I was getting some seriously mixed messages about my future with the organization.

As the weeks passed, I heard that things weren't looking good for Zinta, so I decided to visit her at home. As I approached her porch, I could see her waiting for me behind the screen door. I immediately saw that the disease was getting the best of her. My heart sank.

I had brought her a fruit basket, and she thanked me. She offered me some tea, and we sat down and started talking about her treatments. She seemed defiant and confident in her ability to fight her disease, but she quickly changed the subject. She wanted to know how I was doing. At first, I kept things superficial; I was there to talk about her. But she kept pressing, so I opened up and shared my experiences, my frustration, and my confusion.

Then she started talking. She began to confide in me and told story after story of her experiences as a manager. She described at length the petty office politics, the discouraging atmosphere, and the lack of genuine trust among her fellow managers. She described her regular battles with upper management, who resisted her every effort to make the organization better. I could feel her anguish and sense of disappointment. Then she said something that took me by surprise. She said, "You know, Vince, I've always taken care of my health. I've never smoked a cigarette in my life, and I have no history of lung cancer in my family. I believe the disease I'm fighting today is a direct result of all the stress I have experienced being a manager in this organization."

I was stunned. As I left Zinta's house I grieved for her. I felt angry about why she had to endure what she did. As the days passed, I couldn't get Zinta's words out of my mind. I started to wonder what they meant to me and whether I would ever be prepared to pay the price she had paid.

Two weeks after my visit I received an envelope in the mail from Zinta. When I opened it, I found a card thanking me for the visit and the fruit basket. There was also a letter folded inside, and here's what it said:

Vince,

I understand you may have received a mixed message recently regarding your objectives. Success is a funny thing. Like physics, every action has a positive and negative reaction. On one hand, success has the effect of giving one a sense of achievement, pride in the accomplishment, affirmation of skills, and promotes a desire to expand to the next horizon.

The other side is the reaction from others. Some will rejoice in your achievements. Others, perhaps because of their own insecurities, will feel threatened. These people will inadvertently or purposefully make moves to discourage you, undercut the significance of your success, or redirect you to paths that are less threatening to them. Some people are jealous of others' success. (Why does he get all the "breaks"?) Little do they realize that opportunities exist for everyone.

The choice remains yours. Which of the above will influence you? I encourage you to always be the best you can be and take advantage of opportunities as you find them. You have everything to gain.

Hope this helps,
Zinta

When I think about what it means to be a leader, I think about Zinta and her letter. In the midst of her struggle to survive, she took the time to reach out to a young colleague who needed some encouragement.

Zinta died two weeks after I received this letter, and the organization died along with her. That was the moment I learned that although one leader can make a difference, one lone leader can't sustain culture change on his or her own. Weeks and months after, I reflected on Zinta and her experience. I had many questions. Was her cancer really a result of the stress she endured in that organization? I don't know for sure. But she believed it was so strongly that it must have had some effect on her health.

If things were so bad for her, why didn't she just leave? Over the years, I've been surprised to find how many leaders have lived in working environments almost as bad as the one Zinta put up with. I also discovered the one common factor—they were all baby boomers. I learned that this generation grew up expecting to persevere and put up with whatever they had to, no matter how bad it was. So if you worked for a boss who was a jerk, you put up with it. If you worked in a dreadful work environment, like Zinta did, you put up with it. In a weird sort of way, putting up with all the bullshit was like a badge of honor for many boomers.

I knew I was wired differently than Zinta. That letter forced me to reflect very early on in my career on two important questions: What is leadership, and is it worth dying for?

I learned from Zinta's example that I wasn't prepared to sacrifice the way she had, not for an organization that didn't deserve it—not for an organization that didn't aspire to greatness. An organization like that doesn't deserve the commitment and energy of its employees. That was as clear to me 25 years ago as it is today.

Zinta's experience also taught me that there isn't an artificial division between our work lives and our personal lives. We each have one life, and there's no reason to spend it in a dreadful organization led by uninspiring managers and leaders. Moreover, for most of us, our work is a big part of our lives. We spend a lot of time at work, and for the majority of us it's the main way we contribute to society. So I believe it's critical that we make it the best experience we can. And if we do, we all win—employees, customers, shareholders, our families, and our communities. Organizations make our world work. We need them to be strong and vibrant, not uninspiring and soul-destroying. And it all begins with leadership.

At the time I worked with Zinta, people didn't really talk about leadership. It was all about management, and being a good manager was about doing what you were told and ruffling as few feathers as possible. Twenty-five years after Zinta died, I've decided to start sharing her story because I believe we need to do a lot better when it comes to leadership.

Zinta's letter changed the way I thought about my life's work. It also changed my life in a more practical sense: It inspired me to start my own consulting business. I didn't realize it then, but Zinta challenged me to make a critical decision—a leadership decision.

What I also didn't realize at the time was that the moment I made that decision, I began a quest: *to learn how we can create compelling organizations with leaders who truly inspire others to succeed.* I wanted to find and work with like-minded individuals who aspired to create something special in the organizations they led. Unfortunately, finding those people would not be easy.

When I started my consulting business, I focused on providing private career counseling services to professionals. My work with these clients was gratifying. They began to invite me into their organizations to deliver workshops for their employees. I quickly found I enjoyed that work even more. I also learned that although career counseling let me have an impact at an individual level, leading seminars gave me the opportunity to have an organizational impact. This really appealed to me. And over time, I began to shift my business, relying less on the individual career counseling and more on the work I did inside organizations.

All the projects I worked on had one thing in common: change. I continually worked with organizations, individual leaders, teams, and business units that needed to change but didn't know how. I learned that even people and groups who want change tend to resist it.

As my work grew more complex and strategic in nature, I decided I needed to learn more about organizational development, leadership, and change. This is when I began to pursue my graduate degrees. I kept running my business while I was in school, and I found being part of these two worlds fascinating. Often the two worlds came together. I would be reading about leadership theories and then testing them out with my clients. I learned which ideas really were valuable and which were theoretically interesting but not connected to the real world. This was the moment I learned to always favor practical, actionable ideas.

My graduate courses made me think about my client work differently. I started to see organizations in a more systemic way. The more I learned, the more I could see what got in the way of organizations' success. I started to focus on what has become the central theme of my career: holistic ways of thinking about business and leadership. My professors were mainly focused on holistic thinking in education, but I was kind of a misfit in my courses. I was self-employed, working with private sector organizations, while my fellow students worked in education, health care, or the public sector. This was the moment I learned that exposure to ideas from other fields can be immensely valuable. Being a misfit is perfectly fine; in fact, it may help you in ways you don't even appreciate at first. I eventually did my doctoral research on what I termed *holistic leadership*. I found leaders who shared a common way of thinking about leadership and how to build compelling organizations. They became my research participants and my teachers. They became my beacon for hope.

I needed that hope, because my quest to work with leaders who aspired to greatness was starting to feel a little naïve.

Why Are Some Leaders Such Jerks?

I worked with one company led by a chief executive officer (CEO) who someone described to me as the "classic asshole." Larry was a savvy business leader, but he was also an arrogant and pompous individual. To make matters worse, he used fear and intimidation as his primary approach to leadership. People in that organization said that every time they interacted with Larry, they left feeling demeaned and deflated.

Human resources (HR) brought me in to run a leadership development program for mid-level and senior leaders. Larry was in one of my initial interviews, and I remember that within five minutes he set an adversarial tone. He went on a rant trashing HR and made it clear he was just putting up with this program. He didn't believe they needed it. When I asked him to describe his approach to leadership, he said quite simply, "It's easy. Fear. Your people have to fear you if you're going to be effective."

Once I started running the program, a lot of people wanted to talk about Larry. His senior leaders struggled with his style, but he was the boss. I told them that they had a responsibility to give Larry honest feedback. It would help him become a better leader. But nobody wanted to speak up. So they put up with him, and Larry continued to be the classic asshole.

I ended up working with this organization through one of the biggest crises they had ever faced. A major supplier went through a nine-month strike, crippling my client. However, the leaders really stepped up and kept the organization going. They were struggling. They didn't achieve their financial goals, a failure they weren't used to. But they managed to keep the company profitable, which was an amazing accomplishment in light of the crisis.

The leaders I worked with felt pretty good about themselves after the crisis was over. The company even got positive media attention for the way they managed the situation. I also saw how the leaders came to trust one another more and work together better. It was an important insight: Adversity can tear you apart or make you stronger. In this case, it made the leaders stronger.

Unfortunately, about a week after the crisis was over, the senior leadership had a meeting with Larry. They were all expecting him to congratulate them for managing so well. Well, he didn't. He told them they were lucky to pull through, and he proceeded to point out all the times they had dropped the ball during the strike. When I talked to the leaders about this meeting, some of them had tears in their eyes. I heard them out and then asked, "Why didn't any of you stand up to Larry?" Complete silence filled the room.

I told them that leaders need to have the courage to call out bad behavior, no matter where it comes from. It's about speaking truth to power. It's not easy, but it is necessary at times. They told me that no one stood up because they were afraid—afraid of what Larry could do, afraid that they would lose their jobs. I felt for them. It was difficult to watch grown men and women talk about being belittled like that.

I felt obligated to talk to Larry about his behavior, but I knew he would retaliate. He would end my contract, but that didn't bother me. I was more concerned that if I confronted him, he would make things worse for his leaders and I didn't want that to happen. Things were already bad enough for them. My contact in HR told me not to bother. He said the leaders would have to come to terms with Larry in their own ways. And over the next few months, they did—a few of them resigned, but most just put their heads down and kept putting up with it.

This experience weighed on me for quite a while. I kept asking myself what I could have done differently. But in the end, the real questions were: Why do organizations put up with leaders like Larry? Why does it seem that there are so many people like him out there? What are they trying to achieve? That company was very successful; it is possible to drive success through fear and intimidation, but that strategy can only get you so far. Leaders like Larry get the worst of their people. They waste the human potential of their teams. So much potential is left unrealized. So much potential is destroyed.

This is the moment I learned that to change organizations, you need a little bit of naïve optimism. You have to believe in the potential of leaders and employees and what they can do to create great organizations. However, great leaders and great organizations are unfortunately the exception. The real work is in helping all those other leaders and organizations to be better. My personal resolve got stronger. I became even more committed to my quest.

Why Are Many Leaders So Lame?

A little later in my career, I worked with a technology company whose founder and CEO, Jim, was a brilliant guy. He designed software for the financial services industry, and he was successful within this niche. Customers came knocking on his door. His company grew quickly. But as a leader, he was a little rough around the edges. He could be hard on his people, but everyone knew his intentions were good, so it didn't bother them that much.

By the time I was brought in to build a leadership program, the company was struggling. New competitors had entered the market, and the company's software was starting to look dated. They had become complacent. Success had made them lazy. Talking to employees in the company, I learned that product development staff never talked to those in marketing, and marketing staff never talked to those in sales. Sales leaders were in the field promising release dates for new versions of the software, creating customer demand for a product that nobody was actually building inside the organization. It was a mess.

The leadership forums I designed and ran were difficult meetings. The leaders only wanted to sit around and blame one another for the company's problems. They were too focused on their own small silos—they weren't operating as a whole unit.

When the business had been doing well, the dysfunction didn't seem to matter—everything was easy. Cash kept streaming into the company. However, success can create a false sense of security and a false sense of how good you really are. That's what happened here and that's when I learned that the numbers don't always tell the whole story.

Now that sales were lagging, everyone had noticed the cultural and organizational problems, but nobody knew what to do about them. Jim was at a loss, and the other leaders were stressed out, realizing that they were the ones who were going to have to figure out how to save the company. They were all under great pressure to turn things around. But they weren't responding. They were inept. They were helpless.

One day after a meeting with this group, I went to the parking lot and put my computer bag and materials in my car. As I went to shut the trunk, I looked up at the client's office building. I saw the floors where my client had offices. I pictured all those leaders who spent all their time fighting with one another, and then I pictured all the other floors with other companies in that office building, each one playing out its own self-created drama. It was only from outside the building that you could see how small those fights were, how much they distracted everyone and how much they got in the way of success. This is when I began to understand that to create a strong organizational culture, you need to begin with a strong leadership culture.

In my experience, many organizations had pretty weak leadership cultures. Some were even dreadful and others were completely dysfunctional. What's important to understand is that they were made that way, often by default because a few leaders paid attention to this thing called leadership culture.

However, I did find that there were a few truly exceptional leaders that had figured it out. They deliberately built strong leadership cultures in the organizations that they led. I was fortunate to work with a few of those leaders. They showed me that leadership culture can be a powerful and positive force in organizations. But it is also fragile. And the moment you stop paying attention to it, things can begin to erode.

In the end, I also learned that we all have a choice. We don't have to put up with uninspiring or toxic leadership cultures. We can create great ones. But it takes concerted effort to build and sustain them over the long term. It means you have to be relentlessly focused on keeping the cultures strong. It all begins with an aspiration for great leadership.

At that point in my journey, I also thought a lot about the quest I was on. I realized that as a consultant, I would always be on the sidelines, helping my clients but not really creating cultures myself. I enjoyed consulting, but I wanted to help build a business, too. I didn't just want to be a leadership expert—I wanted to be a leader. So I decided that I needed to go back into an organization, to take everything I learned from 10 years of consulting work, my graduate programs, and my research, and see if I could actually make a strong leadership culture happen within a company.

Has Anyone Noticed That We've Stopped Talking about Our Values?

I never would have expected that my next opportunity would emerge so quickly. I was approached by a search firm to consider a role with a new start-up pharmaceutical company. The CEO, John, was an industry veteran. He had left a senior marketing job with a top-tier pharmaceutical company to start this new venture. He also had a vision for creating a different kind of pharmaceutical company.

John had a great vision for the culture he wanted to create, and it was distilled in five core values. These really attracted me to the organization. I decided to make the leap and became responsible for leading the learning and leadership function. It was a great experience with a great group of people. I had the opportunity that I was looking for: to go into a company and set my ideas into action. The good news was that John (and everyone else) wasn't looking for the same old ways of working.

As a new company, we were pushing ourselves to think and act differently in all areas of our business. One of the things John taught me was a very subtle and important insight about leadership. John always believed that many leaders never really understand how a company actually makes money. He thought that was the cornerstone of all leadership, because once you understand that basic fundamental, it then drives all your behavior as a leader. This time is when I began to learn about the deep connection between strategy and leadership.

Over the three years I was there, a subtle change took place in the conversations we were having about our company. In the early days we spent a lot of time talking about our values and the kind of culture we wanted to create. We were very successful at doing that. But then we stopped having those discussions.

Once in an all-staff meeting I shared my personal observation, "Has anyone noticed that we've stopped talking about our values?"

It was a question that resonated with many. What I would learn later when I was back in consulting was that organizations tend to do this. Values and culture are closely connected to each other. Companies sometimes treat them as a project, something to be checked off the list. I would see this faulty thinking over and over again. Culture building isn't a onetime project or a simple to-do item; rather, it's never ending. You have to constantly work on it. If you don't, it will begin to erode.

Although my experience at this company was great and my team and I accomplished some really good things, I still felt I was not fully involved in the business. As a leader of a support function, I still felt one step removed from truly being involved. In just three years, I had already started to move into maintenance mode, and I knew that wasn't where I excelled. It was time to move on.

All along, the spirit of Zinta was still present as my inspiration. Then the chance I was really looking for finally arrived. I joined another consulting firm that was soon acquired by a new company called Knightsbridge Human Capital Solutions.

How Do You Create a Vibrant Culture?

Knightsbridge was founded by David Shaw, a seasoned business leader who had a strong track record as a corporate CEO. David had an idea: He wanted to give organizations a more integrated way to address their human capital needs at every stage, from recruitment, selection, and talent attraction to employee and leadership development. Optimizing the productivity of their people and addressing their career management and outplacement needs were also concerns. His idea was ambitious but untested. David also stressed the importance of not only building a great professional services firm but also becoming a great operating company. This dual part of our vision created a healthy tension in our organization. However, David and the rest of the Knightsbridge employees were committed to making this goal a reality.

All of this work was exciting enough, but even better, David didn't just talk about the business model he envisioned; he also talked about building a vibrant company culture. He knew that both would be critical to our success. And I knew that my vision of an integrated leadership practice would help play a role in making his overall vision a reality. I had found my opportunity to be the leader and put all my ideas about leadership and culture in place both within my business and externally with our clients.

Building a different type of consulting firm like Knightsbridge started with hiring a different kind of person. We wanted people who naturally focused on serving clients. We needed people who could put their egos aside and who could be polished, yet down to earth. They needed to be smart but humble, passionate but not willing to let the ends justify the means. They needed to be optimists. And because we wanted to grow quickly, we needed people who were subject matter experts but who also had an entrepreneurial, risk-taking spirit. We named this unique set of qualities the K-Factor,[1] and I've always made the K-Factor a priority for myself as a leader and within my own practice area of Knightsbridge.

I've learned that for any organization, the culture is both what binds you together and what propels you forward—but only if you get it right. If you don't, your culture becomes your fatal flaw. What I also learned was that, for a professional services business like Knightsbridge, culture has a real impact on the customer's experience.

In my time at Knightsbridge, I held several roles of increasing responsibility. Then in July 2008, I was given the opportunity I was looking for: David asked me to lead a new Leadership Practice. My job was to integrate three existing and separate businesses and redefine how we went to market. It was a great opportunity, and I immediately noticed something in me begin to change. As an executive I now felt a greater sense of responsibility and accountability—more than at any other time in my career. I felt a direct obligation to our shareholders and board. I felt an even greater sense of accountability to our customers and employees. I was thrilled to have such an exciting opportunity to take on— but I also knew it would take hard work to succeed. I knew this move was a personal turning point for me.

But something happened in July of that year that would truly test my leadership: the financial crisis of 2007–2008.

As my team and I were busy working to redefine the Knightsbridge Leadership business, some of our clients began to put leadership projects on hold. They, like every other company, were struggling for their survival. Yet, during this time, I also had other clients respond very differently to the same conditions. Although they too were affected by the financial crisis, they didn't put leadership development on hold. In fact, they invested in it even more. They realized that to weather this crisis, their leaders would need to be at their strongest, and the organization needed to support them. It was amazing to see the contrast in approach and response to this challenging situation.

As you might imagine, this was a very stressful time for all leaders. Knightsbridge fared well because our business model was tested and it was strong. Having a holistic business model with a collection of practice areas that can survive changes in economic cycles was a significant benefit for us. It was part of David's vision for the company and it worked. It was also a big personal test for me. I learned that as a leader, you personally need resilience and resolve in difficult times. Not only do you need to manage your own reactions in those situations, but you also need to manage those of your team. And in our case, we also needed to be there for our clients in their time of need. It was our collective obligation at Knightsbridge. We stood by those who were struggling to deal with the fallout of the financial crisis. Many of our clients lost their jobs. We needed to be there for them, and our career transition and outplacement services helped these clients in their time of need. Others who managed to keep their jobs were working hard to make sure their companies remained intact during the crisis.

What we also learned was that many of our clients, particularly those who were new executives, had led only in good economic times. For them, this was their first experience leading through what would be one of the toughest economic periods in history. Our services became invaluable as we supported our clients through the crisis. I was proud of my colleagues and the impact they had on our clients during this difficult period.

My team and I took to heart the now famous words of Rahm Emanuel, who in the middle of the financial crisis said, "You never want a serious crisis to go to waste. And what I mean by that is an opportunity to do things you think you could not do before."

We didn't waste this crisis.

Instead, we introduced a completely new go-to-market strategy called the Leadership Pathway. It provided our clients with a more integrated and strategic approach to leadership effectiveness and leadership continuity. Although the recession was hard on many companies, we came out stronger and better positioned to meet the obligations we had to our clients. What was also important to us was an idea I always believed in strongly: *We couldn't just preach this leadership stuff; we needed to live it ourselves.* We needed to work both to become great leaders and to model great leadership when working with our clients. If we did, they would notice and feel the difference, and in turn we would have greater impact through our work with them. I can say that we have accomplished this aspiration because we were able to build a strong leadership culture within my team. The other lesson is that building a strong leadership culture isn't just a destination you arrive at. You must remain committed in your efforts to sustain it.

In some ways, I feel that I have been fortunate to have carried out Zinta's vision from all those years ago. Unfortunately, she was trying to change an organization that didn't want to change. She worked in a toxic leadership culture. I know I'm lucky to be at a company like Knightsbridge where growth and change is the expectation and where we share a collective aspiration to build a truly great organization. I never take that fact for granted, because I have learned over the years how rare this achievement can be.

And that's the final lesson of my leadership story: Don't waste your time in an organization that doesn't deserve your investment. Remember Zinta. You aren't just investing your time or your career—you're investing your life.

So as a leader, you need to determine whether your organization is worthy of that investment. If it is, then roll up your sleeves and get busy making it the best organization it can be. Your organization desperately needs you and your personal leadership. It needs you to make the leadership decision to become a great leader. It needs you to step up to your obligations as a leader. It needs you to tackle the hard work that you must do as a leader. It needs you to build a strong community of leaders in your organization. Are you ready?

Reflect—Your Personal Leadership Story

As you reflect on the ideas in this chapter, think about your answers to the following questions:

1. What is your personal leadership story?
2. What critical leadership experiences have shaped you as a leader?
3. What were the positive experiences that had an impact on you?
4. What were the negative experiences that had an impact on you?
5. Who can you share your personal leadership story with?
6. How might you help a fellow leader better understand his or her own personal leadership story?

CHAPTER 2

What's Wrong with Leadership Today?

During the 2012 U.S. presidential race, the Republican Party attempted to paint a picture of Barack Obama as an ineffective leader who let down the American people. They did this by using the metaphor of an empty chair leader. Then the *New Yorker* picked up on the metaphor and ran a cover showing Republican candidate Mitt Romney at a presidential debate standing next to an empty chair. The cover struck a nerve with readers. E-mails flowed in. Some readers were outraged, believing the image to be disrespectful to the office of the president. Others were strongly supportive, believing it was time to call out poor leadership.

What was particularly telling about this cover was the strong reaction that readers of the *New Yorker* had to the metaphor of empty chair leadership. In fact, I believe it is a common human response. We all react viscerally when our leaders don't perform the way they should—when they don't fill their chairs effectively—and hold a title but don't really lead. We are filled with a sense of disappointment and even despair. In the worst cases, we become disillusioned.

At the same time, we all hope to be great leaders, to be led by great leaders, and to be part of the great organizations that we collectively build. But too often our leaders let us down. Many fail to live up to the obligations of the role. If we are honest with ourselves, we all know that stories of great leaders leading great companies act as beacons of hope, but these stories are the minority. More common are stories of empty chair leaders—those who are inept or motivated solely by personal ambition.

When Organizations Let Us Down

On March 14, 2012, Greg Smith's article "Why I Am Leaving Goldman Sachs" was printed in the *New York Times*. It was his resignation letter. In it he described how the culture of Goldman Sachs had become toxic and destructive. He argued that the company had lost its moral fiber by building a culture that valued making money at any cost, even at the expense of the quality of client service and client relationships.

Smith was most frustrated with the way the company thought about making money and how it viewed its clients. He said that when he first joined the company 12 years prior, the culture was built on teamwork, integrity, humility, and always doing right by clients. Goldman Sachs saw its culture as its secret sauce, and that's what made it one of the world's largest investment banks.

Smith said he knew it was time for him to leave the organization when he could no longer look at prospective young employees and tell them that it was a great place to work.

He hoped his public resignation would be a wake-up call to the board of directors of Goldman Sachs and to directors of other companies in the financial services industry. His basic plea to all these companies was to make the client the real point of focus again. He advised boards to aggressively weed out morally bankrupt employees, no matter how much money they might be making. He said Goldman Sachs needed to get its culture right again so people could work for the right reasons.

Smith's resignation letter went viral, becoming a worldwide trending topic on Twitter. This story clearly struck a nerve within the industry and with the general public. But not everybody saw it the same way. At one extreme were people who saw Smith as a hero, someone with the courage to stand up and tell it like it is in the morally corrupt financial services industry.

At the other extreme were insiders in investment banking who saw Smith as nothing more than a disgruntled employee. These insiders knew Goldman Sachs was a tough place to work, and if after 12 years you rose only to a mid-level vice president position (as Smith did), then you didn't have what it took to succeed. To these insiders, this story was about an individual who couldn't make partner and who was out to tarnish the reputation of the company.

When I first read about Smith's public resignation, I was quite surprised. Given the work I do, I love to follow the stories of great companies, and Goldman Sachs had always been one of them. I had followed the company only from afar, but I knew about its strong financial performance, its impressive list of alumni, and the many business and industry awards it has earned over the years. This company has been on Fortune's list of the "100 Best Companies to Work For" every year since the magazine first launched it. It's also been on Fortune's list of the "World's Most Admired Companies" and Barron's list of the "World's Most Respected Companies."

I had also admired the company's commitment to leadership development. A February 16, 2010, Bloomberg *BusinessWeek* article described Goldman Sachs's commitment to growing its next generation of leaders. The company had classroom-based programs, external assignments, coaching, seminars, and a Leadership Acceleration Initiative for high-potential managing directors. The firm's leadership believed that the team was more valuable than the individual high performer and that the firm was more important than the team. That commitment to the team over the individual star performer would set the firm apart from its competitors. The article also pointed out that Goldman Sachs made the list at a time when financial services companies were reeling from the financial crisis. Even through the downturn, the company preserved its core leadership development efforts.

I have worked with people from many other organizations who envied Goldman Sachs's commitment to developing leaders. I always believed that Goldman Sachs got it as a company. Goldman Sachs was a sign of hope, a standard for other companies to look up to. It was an example I would point to in discussions with other organizations.

But despite these great accomplishments, Goldman Sachs has also been embroiled in several high-profile litigations and scandals as a result of employee misconduct. The string of controversies has tarnished its reputation.

How does this happen? How can a company as great as Goldman Sachs, one we could point to as an exemplar for others, find itself in this position, with litigations, scandals, and Smith's resignation letter all eroding its good name?

Apparently even our greatest companies can and will let us down. It's enough to make anyone lose hope. And this is where the Goldman Sachs story becomes more universal. It's not just about Goldman Sachs. You can insert the name of many other companies in its place, and the story is the same. We as leaders can't ignore what is happening. We need to work together to bring back a sense of hope about leadership. But before we can do that, we need to really understand where we are failing. We need to face the harsh realities that leadership has become disconnected, disappointing, and disgraceful.

Leadership Is Disconnected

I talk to many leaders in my work, and many tell me they feel like they are working in isolation. As leaders, many of us are disconnected from our employees, our peers, and our colleagues. Each one of us is trying to do our best, but we don't feel supported and don't have a real sense of community with our fellow leaders. A survey of 83 chief executive officers (CEOs) at public and private companies found that half reported feeling a sense of isolation that could hinder their ability to effectively carry out their jobs.[1] The survey also found that first-time CEOs were particularly vulnerable: 70 percent of new CEOs reported feeling lonely in their roles.

Although this research focused on CEOs, I believe this experience is more widespread. It's not just lonely at the top. It's lonely throughout all leadership ranks.

We should acknowledge that leadership roles by their nature do impose a sense of separation. Leaders need to do difficult things at times. They need to hold poor performers accountable, make decisions to close down companies, and fire people. Even when these actions are necessary, they serve to distance leaders and cut them off from others. That's a reality. We should also acknowledge that in large organizations, leaders often don't know one another. They're so busy they rarely have time to connect and build relationships.

But our leadership experience doesn't have to be so isolating. We certainly don't get the best from our leaders this way.

Consider the story of Simon, a young product manager who worked in a pharmaceutical company. Simon was smart, well liked, and very good at his job. As soon as the senior leaders noticed him, they promoted him. Suddenly, Simon was now responsible for the company's most successful and profitable product.

For a while, things went really well. Simon excelled in his new role. For about a year and a half, sales and market share were strong. Simon became *the golden boy*. He was held up as a model of what other workers should aspire to become. Other product managers were measured against him. He got a lot of positive attention and adulation.

Then the trouble started. A competitor launched a new product at a dramatically discounted price. It surprised everyone; the market in that therapeutic area had changed overnight. Simon was now under a lot of pressure to come up with a response. No matter what he tried, nothing seemed to help. He started to feel isolated and unsupported. He was no longer the golden boy. He quickly realized he wasn't being invited to the same meetings any longer. He was purposely being cut off. He knew it, and so did everyone else.

Unfortunately, Simon wasn't able to come up with a solution that worked. Market share took a significant hit, and six months later, Simon was fired. The company believed that Simon had failed them. And to some extent, they were right: He did fail to meet that unexpected challenge.

Simon also failed because he began to believe all the hype that was being generated about him. He quickly went from hero to zero. But I also believe that the company failed Simon. Management was mesmerized by their new star, but they failed to support him when he needed it the most. Maybe they promoted him too quickly. Maybe they focused too much on the short-term results he was getting and didn't bother to show him how to translate his initial success into a sustainable long-term plan. Simon became isolated because his company didn't support him.

Leadership Is Disappointing

You don't have to look very far to see great examples of leaders who disappoint us. It could be that sense of disappointment when we read of corporate leaders who have behaved badly or bilked their company and shareholders out of millions. It could also be that moment when you are in the voting booth during an election, looking at the slate of candidates, and you are left asking yourself: Is this the best we could do? In these situations, it seems we are disappointed before we even elect our politicians—even before they take office and really begin to disappoint us.

For the vast majority of us, disappointing leadership also occurs in more personal ways. This has become apparent to me over and over again in my work with leaders.

A couple of years ago, in one leadership development program, Nate struggled during the first three days of the program. He was resisting everything and didn't want to be there. Then something changed in him when he completed a Personal Leadership Timeline activity.

As participants were busy working away, I noticed at one point that Nate was just sitting there. I assumed he was still resisting and choosing not to participate in the activity. When I approached him, however, I realized he was deep in thought. He shared with me that one of the patterns he had observed over his personal leadership timeline was that every negative experience in his career came about when he worked for a boss who was a jerk. One such boss in particular was very difficult and would routinely yell, scream, and belittle employees. Nate said he remembered how it always eroded his personal sense of engagement as an employee.

Then he asked himself the very question that caused him to really think hard about his own approach to leadership. He said, "I just wondered, if my team was completing this activity, where would I show up as their leader? Would I be viewed as a leader creating a positive experience or a demoralizing one?"

It now became clear to me why Nate was so deep in thought. He realized in that moment how his employees viewed him. Nate understood for the first time that he was probably the jerk on their personal leadership timeline and he didn't like that reality at all. At that moment something changed in Nate. He became completely engaged in the program. He stopped resisting because he realized he didn't want to be the leader who demoralized his team and colleagues. He no longer wanted to be the leader he had become.

This is an important insight for leaders like Nate to gain, because emerging research suggests there is a price to pay if you are a jerk and a disappointing leader. An infographic in *Inc.* magazine recently focused on "The Real Productivity-Killer: Jerks."[2] It synthesized the findings of several studies on the real costs of lame leadership and bad bosses. For example:

- Seventy-five percent of employees report that their boss is the worst and most stressful part of their job.
- Sixty-five percent of employees would take a new boss over a pay raise.
- Fifty percent of employees who don't feel valued by their boss plan to look for another job.
- Thirty-three percent of employees with bad bosses confess to not putting in maximum effort.
- Twenty-nine percent took sick days when they were not ill.

Even worse, bad leaders are bad for your health. Employees who have poor relationships with their bosses are 30 percent more likely to suffer from coronary heart disease. Maybe Zinta was right after all. Her disease may well have been a function of being in that dreadful organization led by lame and bad bosses.

As leaders, we never want to hear that we are disappointing our employees. It's certainly not something I want to hear. But it's important for us to be honest with ourselves so we can stop letting everyone down.

When you are a disappointment as a leader, you erode the engagement of your followers. They won't go the extra mile for you or your organization. They will never give you their full discretionary effort. Think of your own personal experience when you have worked with a disappointing leader. There's a good chance that you never gave that leader your best. In fact, there's a good chance you purposely withheld your discretionary effort.

As I've shared this idea with other leaders, it seems I've somehow uncovered a secret that we are all carrying—one that all employees carry. We all consciously withhold a part of ourselves when we're stuck with a boss that disappoints us. It's not how we want to behave, but it's how we are forced to behave in the face of lame and disappointing leadership.

I believe this is the price that organizations pay when they have empty chair or mediocre leaders. Your employees come to work each day thinking: *How much effort do I really want to put in today? Is my boss worth my full engagement?*

For this reason, organizations have a chronic problem with employee engagement. Only one in five employees is ever fully engaged. Although we know that working for an admired leader is the number one nonmonetary motivator of employees, we don't seem to appreciate the impact bad leadership has on engagement. Empty chair leaders create unmotivated employees. The employee experience is a function of the quality of the leadership experience.

As a leader, you need to understand the price being paid in your organization for having disappointing leadership.

Leadership Is Disgraceful

Leadership today has also become disgraceful. You don't have to look very far to see that many leaders have lost their way. It's all over the front page: Enron, Lehman Brothers, the global financial crisis, the Libor scandal. Corruption is everywhere. And many of the leaders at the center of these stories seem to walk away free and clear—with big severance packages. How is this possible?

Our leaders have let us down. Employee trust and confidence in senior leadership, organizations, and boards of directors have been in a steady decline. The most pessimistic survey results show that only 7 percent of employees have confidence that the senior leaders in their organizations are looking out for their best interests.[3]

Every time I start working with a new client, I ask to look at the most recent employee engagement survey. I look at only one question—the one that asks about employee trust and confidence in senior leadership. I know that if the percentage is low, I immediately have a sense of the scale of the problem. But the problem goes deeper. Not only is there no trust in senior leaders, but trust in business in general has been declining. We are losing faith in our institutions.

Disgraceful leadership has also put boards under fire. Back in 2009, I was at a dinner event for directors. There was a panel discussing the role of boards in the aftermath of the financial crisis. It was a passionate and lively conversation, but I got the sense there was something no one was willing to raise, until one panel member spoke up. She created quite the stir when she said, "You can point fingers at corrupt CEOs, but we have to accept that boards in these companies were asleep. All of this happened under our watch.

Where was our leadership? Where is the leadership of your board today?" Silence filled the room. No one presented a counterargument because everyone knew she was right.

I have learned that scandals can also weaken the leadership culture of a company. We recently launched a large leadership development initiative with an organization. Weeks before the pilot program began, the company came under fire for a financial scandal.

During the program, the leaders of this company discussed the scandal. They talked about the shame they felt being leaders in this organization. You could see it as they sat there with their heads down and shoulders slouched. They looked defeated. They resented being painted with the same brush as the rogue executives who caused the scandal.

When these scandals happen, all of us as leaders are tarnished. I know firsthand that the majority of CEOs whom I have had the privilege of working with take their roles seriously and lead ethically, with integrity and humility. These are the CEOs I admire. They are not the problem. But the few who act in a disgraceful manner erode the trust we need in our leaders. The public just doesn't trust its leaders anymore, and we have to do something about it. We need to collectively find our way back and restore the trust and confidence that people have in us. We have to stop making leadership a disgrace.

How Did We Get Here?

Leadership has become lame in many organizations. Many of the leaders I work with say they feel complacent in their roles because they aren't inspired by the leaders above them. Employees will say that most leaders they have worked with are average at best. And we as leaders know that being an average leader isn't good enough in today's world.

So how did we get here? There are four primary reasons for today's crisis in leadership. The first is that we have become overreliant on a hero model of leadership, always looking to one individual to save us from our problems and challenges. Second, we glorify and worship charisma. We have made celebrities out of our most charismatic leaders, and we even promote jerks as models of great leadership. Third, we have consistently promoted technical superstars into leadership roles. We inadvertently put people not suited for leadership into these roles and hope that they will rise to the challenge. Some do. However, most don't. Finally, we have taken a quick-fix approach to leadership development. We continually jump from fad to fad, thinking that the latest program will solve all our problems.

We Have Relied on the Heroic Model of Leadership

The story of Simon shared earlier in this chapter has been repeated countless times in countless organizations. At the core is a belief in the heroic model of leadership. It's a model we all know too well—the idea that one leader, usually at the top of the organization, has all the answers and can single-handedly lead the way.

This model may have occasionally worked in the past if the person was truly extraordinary, but it certainly won't work in today's complex and uncertain world. The old heroic model of leadership just isn't sustainable anymore. No one leader will have all the answers.

It is risky to put all your faith in just one individual. And when you focus on only one leader at the top, you actually take your attention away from other leaders in an organization. Emerging leaders, mid-level leaders, and executives all contribute to the success of an organization, but if we focus only on the few at the top, we fail to support and grow the leaders we need for the future.

We Have Glorified Charismatic Leaders

Unfortunately, the problem is amplified because we don't just focus on a few heroes at the top; we then turn them into celebrities. Think of all those charismatic celebrity CEOs out there. We adore them. Jim Collins warned against the dangers of charismatic CEOs in his book *Good to Great*. Yet here we are today, still adoring them. In the process we give them too much money and power. I'm not saying that charisma is bad; not at all. All leaders need a certain amount of it, but charisma can have a dark side, too.

Author Geoffrey Nunberg, in his book *Ascent of the A-Word*, dubs this the "age of assholism," because some of the world's nastiest leaders have become the most successful. He cites Steve Jobs as one of the most famous examples. Walter Isaacson, author of the best-selling biography *Steve Jobs*, describes him as a person who succeeded despite being a "colossal asshole." This confirmed my own experience working with these types of leaders over the years. When the Jobs biography came out, many of my clients read it. What I found fascinating was the common response they all had. First, there was a deep sense of admiration for what Jobs was able to build at Apple. I would share that sense of admiration. However, there was also confusion regarding his personality style. Many people I talked to felt let down because the recurring stories of temper tantrums, manipulations, crying, and other petty behavior seemed to erode how Jobs was viewed.

I gained another insight during these discussions about the story of Jobs. I find that leaders have become confused. When we see these kinds of leaders being glorified even though they are jerks, we become skeptical. You ask yourself: Is this what great leadership is about? Do I need to be a jerk to succeed as a leader? If you look at examples in the media, the answer seems to be yes. But most people I work with want to lead in a more positive and optimistic way. And many get confused when they see jerks rewarded and celebrated to the extent that they are. This practice has to stop.

We can all acknowledge that there are times when leaders need to be harsh, because a positive approach does not always get results. Sometimes you need to hold an underperforming worker accountable. Or you need to bring a sense of urgency to a team that is not delivering. Or you are cleaning up a situation after a major screw-up. In these moments, a glimpse of your harsh side can increase motivation, improve performance, and communicate the severity of the situation. Jerks get people's attention. But there's a difference between selectively being harsh when the situation demands it and being a jerk all the time. One's a tactic; the other is a personality trait.

We Have Promoted Technical Superstars into Leadership Roles

Few leaders set out to become lame or even mediocre. However, something has happened in organizations where we've come to tolerate mediocrity from our leaders. From my work, I have found that part of the problem is that we've promoted strong technical performers into leadership roles. Think about your own career. If you're like most leaders, you were really, really good at what you did—whether it was accounting, marketing, engineering, sales, and so on. In fact, you were one of the best. You got rewarded with a promotion to your first management or leadership role. The thinking was that if you were strong technically, you would obviously be strong in a management or leadership role.

And if you are like most leaders I have talked to, you really didn't have much choice in the matter. Moving up into a leadership role was the only way you could make more money, get more prestige, or have more influence. Up was the only way forward.

But when you took the role, you quickly realized that you needed to start dealing with staff issues and important business decisions. And the longer you were in the role, the further away you got from what got you the job in the first place: the technical stuff.

So you went from being a brilliant individual contributor to being thrown into the leadership deep end without a lot of support from your organization. You needed to figure out all the personnel stuff on your own. You needed to understand how your role changed and the expectations you had to live up to. You either sank or learned to swim. But even if you figured out how to swim, you may have just kept your head above water. To cope, you then relegated the people issues to second place and focused on the more stimulating technical parts of your job. Then you became a leader in title but not in action.

Even if you realize that being a leader isn't your thing and you are tired of disappointing yourself and others, it's really difficult to stop. We haven't made it easy for leaders to put up their hands and say, "I'm not good at this. Help me find another way to add value in this company." It takes a pretty big person to admit their weaknesses and give up the perks that come with a leadership role. But until we stop promoting technical stars into leadership roles and stop making it difficult for people to step down, our organizations will continue to be filled with leaders who put their passion for the technical aspects ahead of the leadership demands. In the end, they disappoint us because they don't end up truly leading.

We Have a Quick-Fix View to Developing Leaders

In her book *The End of Leadership*, Harvard professor Barbara Kellerman takes aim at the leadership industry and warns companies to have a "buyer beware" attitude. She argues that this industry hasn't made leaders more effective and ethical—it's done the opposite. She explains that at the root of the problem is a set of mistaken assumptions. For one, we have always thought of leadership as being static. We have also assumed leadership is simple and something that can be easily taught and learned by the masses. And we have overemphasized an individualistic view of leadership, ignoring the context in which leaders lead and the impact it has on their effectiveness.

Furthermore, we have been too simplistic about what it really takes to develop leaders. We are always looking for a quick-fix solution to our problems. Companies jump from fad to fad in leadership development, and the leadership industry is more than ready to deliver whatever the latest quick-fix solution is. In addition, in our world of social media where we now communicate in short blog posts and 140-character tweets, there is a huge temptation for leadership advice to become too simplistic. We are dumbing down leadership training and trying to make it too quick and easy to become a good leader. This will result in too many leaders not understanding what real leadership is about.

I went in once to meet a potential client. As the CEO and I were talking about their leadership challenges, he said, "You know, Vince, I really admire what Jack Welch did at GE. Can you build me a 'Be like Jack' program for our leaders?" He thought that all we needed to do was build the program and "sheep-dip" his leaders and then his problems would be solved. I can't tell you how many times I've had this kind of discussion with senior leaders.

A financial services organization tried a different approach. They were in decline, losing market share, and competitors were poaching key talent. After having an epiphany that a lack of leadership was the problem, they took their most senior business developers and account managers and gave each leadership titles. The hope was that by giving each a leadership title, somehow the individuals would suddenly change and begin to demonstrate the leadership the organization so desperately needed. It didn't work, much to their surprise. We came in and helped them put in place a solid and more robust strategy.

As someone who has been on both sides of the leadership industry, both as a purchaser and as a supplier, I often see in my work parallels to the fads that exist in the fitness and health industry—all those magical pills and wacky exercise equipment sold on late-night infomercials. In the end, they all promote a quick-fix solution to weight loss and health. The reality is, like real physical fitness, leadership takes work and commitment. We need to come to terms with the real, hard work required to be consistently great at the practice of leadership and to drive the sustainable performance of our organizations. The quick fix doesn't stick.

It's Time We Stop Settling—and Start Expecting More

When our experience of leadership is routinely disconnected, disappointing, and disgraceful, we begin to lower our expectations. The scandals get the headlines, but the deeper disappointment and even disillusionment happens every day in more mundane ways, as we work with empty chair leaders who lack vision, who don't inspire, and who appear to be simply going through the motions. We can tell that more and more leaders are unmotivated, unwilling, or unable lead effectively.

The longer we live with ineffective and uninspiring leadership, the more disappointed we become. My concern is that over time we become numb to what is truly happening around us.

As leaders we need to face the harsh reality that leadership has become disgraceful. But do we care anymore? When we experience the isolation of being a leader, we start feeling disconnected. Then we start checking out. When we are disappointed by empty chair leadership, we lose hope and give up. We stop aspiring for great leadership from ourselves or others. And then we settle. As soon as this happens, we stop stepping up as leaders. We become bystanders in our organization. We show up every day and go through the motions rather than truly lead. You may have the title of a leader, but you are not fulfilling your obligations. You may not be inspired by the leadership around you. You think to yourself, "What's the point of stepping up and trying to be a great leader?" The second you have that thought, you have lowered your expectations for yourself and others around you. Seth Godin, in his book *Tribes*, has a powerful thought. He says that settling is a malignant habit. It's a slippery slope. One day you wake up and you've become an empty chair leader.

It is time we stop settling.

It is time we start expecting more from ourselves as leaders.

It is time to start working together to redefine leadership for the future.

That is what the leadership contract is about, and that's what we will explore next.

Reflect—What's Wrong with Leadership Today?

As you reflect on the ideas in this chapter, think about your answers to the following questions:

1. What has been your experience with empty chair leadership?
2. Have you settled and become an empty chair leader?
3. Do you feel disconnected as a leader? Why?
4. What has been your experience with disgraceful leadership?
5. Would your employees say that they give you their full discretionary effort?
6. Are your expectations for leadership high enough for yourself and others?

CHAPTER 3

Why We Need a Leadership Contract

A British game retailer, GameStation, revealed in April 2010 that it legally owned the souls of 7,500 online shoppers.[1] As an April Fools' Day joke, the company had added an "immortal soul clause" to its online contract. The contract read:

> *By placing an order via this Website on the first day of the fourth month of the year 2010 Anno Domini, you agree to grant us a non-transferable option to claim, for now and forever more, your immortal soul. Should we wish to exercise this option, you agree to surrender your immortal soul, and any claim you may have on it, within 5 (five) working days of receiving written notification from gamesation.co.uk or one of its duly authorized minions.*

Luckily for inattentive shoppers, the company decided not to enforce that clause. But it made a useful point. With a simple click, you are actually agreeing to quite a lot. You have some sense that you are bound to a contract, but you don't know in what ways. The same is true when it comes to leadership today.

Our organizations are governed by all kinds of contracts. For a generation, our work lives were dominated by the old employment contract. You know the one: you get a job, remain loyal, do as you're told, and the organization will take care of you until you retire. That contract worked for decades, but we know today that it is no longer valid. But what replaced it?

I believe it's what I call the *leadership contract*. It has actually existed for a while, but most leaders still don't understand its terms and conditions, let alone its fine print.

The Leadership Contract and Its Four Terms

A client of mine, a chief executive officer (CEO), was about to unveil a new strategy he and his executive team had been working on with the board of directors. It was a departure from the past and would require a significant step up in leadership. The CEO and the executive team wanted to make sure leaders in the organization understood the new strategy and, more important, that they understood what it would now mean to lead in the future of that organization. The CEO said, "I need to know that I have leaders who are fully committed to our strategy and to taking their leadership to new levels. I can't have ambivalent leaders who are just going through the motions. Those days are gone."

I explained to them some of the ideas I had been working on about leadership, and they engaged me to set up a process to help their leaders understand these new expectations and reflect on whether they were ready to accept them. In essence, the board members were being asked to understand and accept a set of new leadership expectations for that organization. A new set of terms were established, and leaders needed to sign up.

We should all go through a process like this when we take on new leadership roles. Our organizations need strong leaders to drive success. When you sign the leadership contract, you enter into an agreement: You commit and promise to be the best possible leader you can be for your organization and for your employees. Before you sign up, though, you need to understand the four terms.

Leadership Is a Decision—Make It

Do you aspire to be a great leader? Or are you just going through the motions? The leadership contract demands that you consciously commit to being the best leader you can be. It's no longer good enough to be a great technical leader. It's no longer good enough to be an average leader. Your organization needs you to be a great leader. And it all begins with a decision. Are you ready to make it?

Leadership Is an Obligation—Step Up

Once you truly make the decision to be the best leader possible, you realize that you must now rise to a new standard. You have a higher degree of accountability. You have to fulfill your leadership obligation, to your customers, employees, shareholders, and community. Are you prepared to step up to the obligations of leadership?

Leadership Is Hard Work—Get Tough

You need to commit to tackling the hard work of leadership. You need to have resilience and a real sense of personal resolve to help your company be successful. You will need to set the pace for others in your organization. You can't be a bystander waiting for things to improve on their own. Are you prepared to get tough and do what is necessary to make your organization a success?

Leadership Is a Community—Connect

It's time to stop being disconnected as a leader. You must reach out and build strong relationships with your fellow leaders. You need to commit to building a community of leaders—it all begins with a commitment to connect. Are you ready for it?

■   ■   ■

These four terms go a long way toward addressing the key problems we have with leadership today. We can overcome lame leadership in our organizations when leaders truly understand what it means to be a leader and sign up for the right reasons. It's no longer good enough to be a complacent or ambivalent leader. Your organization needs you to be at your best. Your employees, customers, shareholders, and stakeholders need you to be at your best.

If you accept a promotion without making a conscious decision to become a leader, you won't get the best possible performance out of your team because you will simply be going through the motions.

If you try to be a leader without considering your obligations to the people around you, you won't be focused on your organization's larger goals. You will be thinking about how to advance your own career instead of how to build long-term success. You will make it all about you rather than the obligations you have to others. This creates risk for you and your organization. You might be tempted to do things that get you in trouble as a leader.

If you try to be a leader without digging into the hard work, you won't be prepared for crises. You will be drowning in day-to-day deadlines instead of focusing on where your organization needs to go next. You will find yourself floundering when issues come up on your team because you haven't taken the time to build a collaborative culture. You will leave serious gaps in your team's capabilities because you haven't bothered to tackle the tough issues.

If you try to lead without connecting with other leaders, you will isolate yourself. You will be focusing on your own narrow little world instead of collaborating with peers from across your organization and your community. You will find yourself blindsided by problems you didn't expect because you didn't connect with anyone who could have helped you prepare. You will end up overstressed and overwhelmed because you don't have anyone supporting you.

Leadership is isolating for many of us. We need to understand that leadership is a community. And we have to stop looking for the quick fix. We need to accept that leadership *is* hard work and that we can't avoid tackling the hard problems.

Does any of this sound familiar to you?

Accepting this leadership contract will improve our own working lives, but the benefits don't stop there. I believe that leaders who understand their obligations to those around them won't disgrace themselves with scandal. We have seen too many leaders embarrass themselves and their organizations because they were thinking only about their own short-term interests. We need to hold ourselves to a higher standard. The first step is to really understand the obligations that come with leadership. It's about having clarity, knowing what's expected of you as a leader, and then having the commitment to be the best leader you can be.

That's the essence of the leadership contract. It's not a legal or formal contract. Instead, it is a personal and even moral contract. It's the personal commitment you make to be a great leader—the leader that you must become for yourself, your organization, and for all of us. It's a commitment to redefine how you lead now and to prepare you to be a leader for the future. You bind yourself to this idea and this aspiration. That's what you are signing up for.

Reflect—Why We Need a Leadership Contract

Take a few minutes to reflect on the ideas of this chapter and reflect on the following questions:

1. Think of your leadership experiences and roles for a moment. Did ever you consciously decide to be a leader?
2. Do you lead every day with a sense of clarity regarding your obligations as a leader? Do you know what your obligations are?
3. What is the hard work you face as a leader? Do you have a tendency to tackle the hard work head-on, or do you avoid it?
4. Do you feel disconnected as a leader within your organization? Do you strive to build a sense of community with your fellow leaders?

Leadership Is a Decision—Make It

Several years ago I was working with a group of senior leaders at a large construction company. We were having a lively conversation about leadership when someone asked me, "Hey, Vince, what is leadership?" I said, "Leadership is a decision." It was the very first time I had said those words out loud. It was an intuitive response, in the moment. But right away Earl, one of the participants, snapped, "Well, I never got to make that decision!"

Earl was the senior vice president of engineering services. He had started out as an engineer, but the organization soon offered him a supervisory role and a series of promotions. Earl said that he accepted each of these promotions without thinking about whether he truly wanted a new role or if he was really ready to commit to it.

I looked around the room. Everyone was listening intently. It seemed like Earl's story was striking a chord with the other leaders.

Earl explained that he thought taking on those leadership roles was the logical thing to do. From a practical perspective, it was the only way he could make more money and get more prestige within the company. But he said that every time he took on a more senior leadership role, he moved further and further away from what he really loved to do: engineering.

I have told Earl's story a lot and have been surprised by how many leaders say they've done the exact same thing.

Although making more money, expanding your skills, and having more impact are all somewhat valid reasons to be a leader, they are no longer enough in today's world of business.

Every day you have opportunities to make a leadership decision. But do you answer that call? Many times making the leadership decision to lead isn't easy—it's easier to stay put and play it safe. But staying put makes you an empty chair leader and keeps your organization stuck.

Why Doesn't Anyone Want to Be a Leader Anymore?

I have met a lot of people who relate to Earl's experience, and most of them are about Earl's age. I have also noticed that the younger generation isn't as willing to take on a leadership role just for perks or prestige.

My team and I worked with a software company a while back to design and deliver a two-day leadership program aimed at 30 people they had identified as high-potential leaders. To begin the project, we interviewed these "hi-po" leaders. What we found was quite surprising: The majority of them didn't want the label of a high-potential leader. In fact, leadership had pretty negative connotations for most of them. They thought being a high-potential leader would just mean doing more work. They felt busy enough already, and being saddled with more leadership tasks (including dealing with difficult employee performance issues) certainly didn't appeal to them. They did the math and figured out that all the extra work wouldn't really be reflected in their salaries. And they didn't want to take time away from their families to put in those extra hours. That wasn't a sacrifice they were ready for or wanted to make.

The executive team was pretty surprised—and frustrated—to hear this news. They had assumed everyone would want to be a leader. They figured that these employees would be proud to be tagged with the hi-po leader label. But the more we talked to the hi-pos to figure out why they had such negative views of leadership, the more we realized it was the executive team that was the problem. They were the model for leadership in that company. They all worked 60 to 80 hours per week. They were always on planes traveling the world. When you saw the current executives from afar, as the hi-pos did, all you saw was hard work and personal sacrifice.

The executive team soon realized that they needed to do a better job of demonstrating to the hi-pos all the rewards associated

with the leadership roles—the gratification that comes from serving customers, building great teams, and creating a successful business.

So we changed the focus of the two-day leadership development program. Instead of a launch program, we created a process to help those would-be leaders better understand what a leadership role is really all about—the good, the bad, and the ugly. The participants loved this approach. They were grateful for the chance to decide for themselves whether to step into these new roles. They soon started to realize they had been focusing only on the downsides of leadership. After that two-day event, all but five of our potential leaders decided to continue. Those who opted out did so mainly for personal family reasons but asked to be considered again once their young children were older.

Something is changing in our organizations. Younger employees understand that leadership is a decision and that it needs to be deliberately made. I saw this recently with one of my own team members—a smart, personable guy who had been an informal leader for a while. When his manager and I offered him a formal leadership role, he said, "Wow, I'm really flattered. Thank you so much. Do you mind if I take a couple of weeks to think about it?" Honestly, both his manager and I were a little surprised to hear this. I remember thinking to myself, "Listen, buddy, in my day when someone gave you a leadership opportunity, you just took it. No ifs, ands, or buts." Even I am having a hard time letting go of this outdated perspective on leadership.

We met with him again after the two weeks were up, and this time he said, "Thanks so much for giving me the time to reflect on this big decision. I needed to think carefully about this. Both my wife and I have big jobs, and we also have a young family. I needed to know before committing whether this was the right thing to do for my family. I have thought it through, and I'm in."

I thought to myself, "This guy is much smarter than I was at his age." He knows what it means to be a leader. He appreciates the demands and the pressure. This is why he wanted to make sure that he could really commit to doing the work and becoming a great leader. He took his time to reflect and then made his leadership decision.

Why You Need to Make the Leadership Decision

The first term of the leadership contract begins with the idea that leadership is a decision. There isn't much point in discussing anything else about leadership until we get this clear. Too many theories about leadership just assume that everyone wants to be a leader. But this is a faulty assumption—one that we often are not truly aware that we are making.

We need to replace this faulty assumption with the idea that everyone needs to decide whether they want to be a leader. If we do that, we will end up with leaders who truly want the role and are prepared to do what is necessary to help their organizations succeed. We also help those who don't want the role find other ways to add value in their organizations.

One of the reasons you need to be more deliberate in making leadership decisions is that organizations have changed. In the past, companies were much larger than they are today, with many levels of managerial roles throughout the hierarchy. The good thing was that all those roles acted as effective stepping-stones, enabling individuals to nicely progress from one leadership role to another. Because you could see the stepping-stones ahead of you, each move seemed like a natural and logical step to take and you really didn't have to do too much thinking about the roles you were taking on.

However, companies today are leaner and flatter. The stepping-stones are gone and have been replaced by giant leaps. So when you take on a leadership role in today's world, you don't see the next steps at all. What you do see is a big chasm between your current role and the role ahead of you. It's a significant leap and is one of the primary reasons why there is such a high incidence of failure among leaders assuming new roles.

Much of the research has shown—whether it's at the front line, in the middle, or at the executive ranks—that a significant percentage of leaders derail within a year or two of accepting new roles. I believe it's because they don't deliberately make effective leadership decisions. They don't fully understand what they are taking on and instead make the leap blindly, underestimating the demands and expectations. You may get seduced by the new title, the status, the money, and the perks. You may make assumptions about what leading will really be like but your assumptions may be wrong.

To me, it is a lot like being a first-time parent. No matter how many parenting books you read or how many stories you hear from your friends and family, you can't truly understand it until it's happening to you. And then it hits you—during the 3:00 AM feedings or after your fourth straight sleepless night. Then you know how challenging being a parent really is. The other reason you need to be more deliberate in making leadership decisions is that we've always assumed that everyone wanted to be the leader and we have ended up glorifying leadership roles above others in our organizations. We give leaders more money, more perks, more prestige. But in reality, we've never really let people decide whether they want to take on a leadership role. As a result, I've seen many leaders who don't make the conscious decision to lead. Instead, they just accept the roles they're given. Over time, they become ambivalent or reluctant leaders like Earl. Many feel trapped. They have the title, the prestige, and the money, but the role doesn't excite them. They don't have the passion for leadership.

In his book, *Passion Capital*, author Paul Alofs states that passion is a powerful emotion that leaders use to build lasting value in their organizations. However, without a high degree of passion, you erode your effectiveness as a leader. Without the passion for leadership, you may then find you're always questioning and second-guessing yourself. What you may not fully appreciate is that everyone around you knows it. They can *smell* the indecision, the tentativeness, and the uncertainty you project.

It's important to note that in the past we may have been able to get away with weak leadership because our world was less complex than it is today. We could get by with individuals who didn't make the real decision to be leaders. But things are very different today. Ambivalent or passionless leaders just aren't strong enough to take us through this complex environment. There's too much at stake today. Those who lead solely for personal reasons aren't going to be effective either. We need to make sure that all leaders consciously and deliberately make the decision to lead and make it for the right reasons— we need leaders who bring a strong sense of passion to their roles.

The Two Kinds of Leadership Decisions

Athletes have to make lots of decisions on the field (or on the court or on the ice). In the midst of the action, they have to be able to decide again and again how to move their team closer to victory. Coaches and players can also call a time-out when they believe there is a particularly important decision to be made, one that they can't make in an instant.

Like athletes, leaders also make dozens of real-time decisions in the middle of the action. These small "d" leadership decisions come up many times in a typical day. And then there are the time-out moments. These Big "D" leadership decisions are the critical moments in your career when you have to pause and be more deliberate about the choice you are about to make.

Both types of decisions are important. Big D leadership decisions come at critical times in your career and force you to reflect on who you are as a leader and whether you are ready to take on a new leadership role. Small d leadership decisions are made in the moment and may seem minor compared with Big D decisions, but over time, they can also have a considerable impact on your effectiveness as a leader.

It is important to clarify one point. Leaders make all kinds of decisions, such as where to invest for growth, which suppliers to use, and how to manage customer issues. These are typical business decisions, and there is a lot written about effective decision making for leaders out there.

What I'm talking about here is something more specific. It's those decisions you have to make about your role as a leader both at critical times (Big D leadership decisions) and in the day-to-day experience of leading (small d decisions). These leadership decisions shape how you ultimately show up as a leader. They will also dictate how others will judge your effectiveness as a leader.

Big D Leadership Decisions

In December of 1968, the astronauts on *Apollo 8* were the first humans placed in a lunar orbit. Their primary task was to take photographs of the moon and identify possible landing sites for future missions.

As their spacecraft drifted from behind the moon, they saw the earth rising above the lunar horizon. Astronaut William Anders quickly took a picture of the amazing scene.

The image in his photograph would represent the first time that we were able to look at Earth from space. Up to that point in time, our view of Earth came from maps and globes—images of countries divided by lines and colors. Anders's photograph showed us the planet as it really is—a sphere. Many believe this was a turning point in human history because we fundamentally changed how we viewed ourselves and our planet.

Historians have used the term *turning point* to identify key moments in history, like the *Apollo 8* story, that change the flow of history in a significant manner.

Leaders also experience these moments in their careers where they are about to assume a more senior leadership role. It is important at these critical times that leaders pause and reflect on what they are signing up for.

As leaders, our careers evolve over time. If we are successful, we gain roles of increasing responsibility. Through this journey, we have come to learn that there are four critical times that are particularly important for leaders.

These four leadership turning points demand that you take some time to think about what has changed in your leadership role and, more important, how you must change to be successful as a leader. At each of these four leadership turning points, you must pause and deliberately make a Big D leadership decision.

- The first turning point occurs when those in your organization tell you that they see you as someone with leadership potential. This happened to me when Zinta first told me I had leadership potential. I immediately paused to understand what her words meant to me and what I now needed to do to become a leader.
- The second critical turning point occurs when you take on your first supervisory role. When this happened to me, I quickly realized that from that moment on, I was responsible for others. My focus changed from everything being about me and my performance to supporting the performance of others.
- The third critical leadership turning point is when you assume a mid-level or senior management role. The demands of leadership change considerably, and how you see yourself also must change. When I had one of these roles, I realized that I needed to change my approach to leadership from driving the performance of my team to ensuring I was able to work across the organization with my peers to drive the success of our entire organization.
- The final critical turning point of leadership occurs when you assume an executive role. I recall when I first started my executive role at Knightsbridge. I felt the weight of my obligation to our board and shareholders. My responsibility to my team and colleagues across our company also increased dramatically.

Each of these moments is a turning point in your career. Each represents a significant shift in what is expected of you as a leader. Not only does your role change, but you must change. You must be clear about what is expected of you and the ways in which you must alter how you lead in order to succeed. You can't just jump into the role full of naïve enthusiasm or assume it's another career move.

Instead, you need to pause and make sure that you are clear about the changing demands of the role. You must also be certain whether you are truly prepared to live up to them to ensure that you will succeed when you take the leap. And that is ultimately what a Big D leadership decision is all about. If you don't take a time-out to deliberately make these Big D leadership decisions, you may sign up for something you are not prepared for, and this may affect your ability to succeed in the new role.

Small d Leadership Decisions

Alfred E. Kahn was a highly regarded American economist who was known as the Father of Airline Deregulation. We can thank him and his ideas for all the low-cost airlines like Southwest that have reshaped the airline industry. Kahn was also known for a simply brilliant idea referred to as the "tyranny of small decisions." He wrote an article in the mid-1960s in which he described situations where a number of innocuous small decisions (those that appear small in the moment) cumulatively can result in an outcome that is not desired. In other words, a number of small decisions, each appearing insignificant in the moment and made in isolation of one another, can result in a negative outcome. This simple yet powerful idea has been applied to market economics, environmental degradation, political elections, and health care.

Here's a classic example of the tyranny of small decisions. Imagine a situation where a number of herders graze cows in a common field.[1] Each herder acts independently from one another. They make what they believe is a rational decision to allow their cows to graze freely on the field. They are motivated primarily by their own self-interest. However, what they don't realize is that all the other herders are making the same decision, not fully appreciating the overall impact. Then suddenly one day everyone realizes that the field has been depleted and is no longer suitable for grazing. The small, seemingly easy decision to allow cows to graze without considering the broader implications illustrates why small decisions matter.

This idea also applies to you as a leader, through the many small d leadership decisions that you make (or do not make) countless times each and every day. Although these decisions may appear to be small compared with Big D leadership decisions, they, in fact, play an important role in shaping who you are as a leader. I find, however, that many leaders don't appreciate the importance of these small d leadership decisions.

Consider, for example, Curt, a controller in his organization. His days are constantly filled with too much to do, putting out fire after fire. In these moments when a small d leadership decision needs to be made, Curt knows what he should really do as a leader, but he's too busy to pause and be deliberate. He thinks to himself, "I'll let this one go by this time. I'll make this small compromise just this once." Before he knows it, compromise after compromise has become his regular pattern. He never fully appreciates how his personal leadership effectiveness is eroding and how he is inadvertently letting his team and organization down.

It's in those small moments, when you are under pressure and feeling overworked, that you still have to make the right small d leadership decisions.

Consider a few of the following typical situations that you find yourself in on a regular basis as a leader:

- You are in a meeting and an important issue arises that you disagree with. What do you do? Do you challenge it, or do you let it go?

- A colleague is demonstrating bad behavior that is inconsistent with your company's values. What do you do? Do you provide feedback now, or do you wait for the next opportunity?
- A project in another area of the company is off the rails. No one seems to care. What do you do? Do you confront the issue, or do you ignore it because it's really none of your business?

You may find yourself in countless of these small, almost innocuous moments on a regular basis. In isolation they may not seem that important. It seems logical to you that you can comprise, let the issue go, or ignore it—just this one time. Yet, these small d leadership decisions add up to something truly significant: your identity as a leader. They have an impact on your credibility. They tell your colleagues whether they can trust you—or not.

Now imagine if this is happening not just with you but with other leaders in your organization. Imagine the collective impact of leaders showing up every day and comprising on these small and seemingly harmless situations. You can start to understand why organizations struggle to drive sustained high performance and innovation.

It's time you start taking these small d decisions seriously. It's time you become more deliberate in your decision making so that you don't create the unintended or negative outcomes of failing to make effective small d leadership decisions.

To achieve this goal, when you are leading and confronted with a small d decision moment, what criteria do you use to help you? First, it helps if you have already made the Big D leadership decision. When you have already committed to be the best leader you can be, you are always behaving as the leader. That's the lens through which you are looking day to day, so making small d leadership decisions won't be as challenging. Second, it helps when you are clear on your obligations as a leader (we'll cover this topic in the next chapter). Third, it's also helpful to use your organization's core values to assist you in making effective small d leadership decisions.

Taken together, these three ideas create a powerful and practical approach to help you make effective small d leadership decisions. The next time you find yourself in that moment when a small d decision needs to be made, ask yourself:

- How must I show up as a leader in this moment?
- What is my obligation as a leader in this moment?
- What do my organization's core values dictate that I do in this moment?

Once you can begin to internalize these questions into your day-to-day leadership, you'll find yourself being more deliberate and consistent as a leader. You will provide the necessary leadership that your organization and your team need from you. You will begin to forge a strong reputation as a credible and deliberate leader.

Big D and Small d Leadership Decisions— Clarity and Commitment

Ultimately, Big D and small d leadership decisions both require clarity and commitment on your part. You need clarity about what you're taking on when assuming a leadership role. You need to be clear on the following:

- What's the role really about?
- What are the expectations?
- What will success look like?
- What value must I bring as a leader?
- What impact must I have?

You will also need a strong degree of personal commitment. Ask yourself:

- Am I up for this?
- Am I fully committed to doing what I need to do to make my team and company succeed?

- Am I able to handle the heat that I will be exposed to?
- Am I prepared for the hardships that will come my way?
- Am I committing for the right reasons, or am I doing this only to feed my ego?

Let's go back for a moment and think about the leadership turning points to gain greater clarity as to what changes at each one.

First, you will find at each turning point that the amount of complexity you deal with increases. At times, it may feel like the complexity is increasing exponentially. You have to be able to tolerate ambiguity and the pressure it will impose on you. If you are lucky, you'll be in an organization that will help you through this. But most leaders will need to face this challenge on their own.

Second, you will face considerable scrutiny, which just keeps on increasing across the four turning points. You must be open to it, yet develop a thick skin so it doesn't undermine your confidence as a leader. I believe that the increased scrutiny is a function of the fact that leadership really matters today. There's a lot riding on you—so you better not screw up! First, your peers are scrutinizing you to see if you really are high-potential material. Then your employees analyze your every word and action. Then colleagues across the organization who think you're making their lives harder than necessary, weigh in with their own views of your performance. Finally, board members, customers, analysts, and shareholders will scrutinize your every decision and every move. The spotlight keeps getting brighter.

Third, you will experience regular and ongoing points of realization that make it clear to you: You are accountable. There is no room for excuses as a leader. You must bring the solution, not just the problem. Although obvious enough in concept, it isn't always obvious in practice.

Fourth, you will realize you must demonstrate increasing levels of professional maturity. As an emerging leader, you will find that those around you will want to see you show up as a leader. At the front line you will need to rise above the noise and drama of the people issues and bring a leadership presence. At the middle you will need to be an ambassador of your organization. This implies being levelheaded and having a strong sense of poise. Finally, at the executive or C-suite level, your professional maturity (or lack of it) sets the tone for your entire organization. You will need to have a real executive presence because your personal reputation is tied so closely to your organization's reputation.

You will also come to understand that the degree of impact you must deliver increases dramatically at each turning point. For example, as you become a more senior-level leader, your impact is more widely apparent. The flip side is that so are your mistakes. You will feel a self-imposed sense of urgency to have real impact (or at least you should feel it). You will come face-to-face with your core obligations as a leader, and you will need to take them seriously.

The reason you need clarity and commitment in making Big D and small d leadership decisions is that at each turning point the heat rises, such as the knobs on a gas stovetop. Each knob has a *lo* to *hi* setting, and at each turning point of leadership, the knobs keep turning closer and closer to the highest setting. At every turn, the flame gets higher and hotter—the heat increases. You feel the pressure.

This is why you can't take on a leadership role simply because it feels like the next logical step. This is why you can't jump at an opportunity because it's going to pay you more, give you more perks, or offer a better title on your LinkedIn profile. This is why you can't simply click Agree without understanding what the fine print of the leadership contract is about. This is why you need to pause and truly understand what you are signing up for as a leader, because at each turning point, the pressure and heat increase considerably. In my experience, this is often the fine print of leadership that many never truly fully appreciate.

A Real Leadership Decision Is Visceral

What you will also find when you make the decision to lead is that the change in you will be visceral—you'll feel it and know it, and so will those around you. Leadership will ooze out of every single pore of your body. And when you make both the Big D and small d leadership decisions with clarity and commitment, your game will go to another level. Let's consider a few examples of this visceral change.

When Is a King Not a King?

King George VI of Britain ruled from 1936 to his death in 1952. His story is interesting because he never expected to inherit the throne. In fact, he spent most of his life in the shadow of his elder brother, Edward. When Edward became king, he struggled with the role. He then abdicated the throne to marry Wallis Simpson, an American socialite. Suddenly, George was thrust into a leadership role. He ascended to the throne after considerable controversy when his brother stepped down from the role. George's story was portrayed in the Oscar-winning movie *The King's Speech*. It shows King George VI struggling to fulfill his role. He has a stuttering problem that affects his personal confidence and his ability to speak clearly in public, and it holds him back. George is indecisive and tentative—he is the king in name only. But he manages to change that. Near the end of the movie he must deliver his first wartime speech. Given his speech impediment, delivering such a critical speech at that moment in England's history is extremely important for him and for his country. Although he is under tremendous pressure, he succeeds and delivers a powerful speech. The reaction is overwhelmingly positive.

As he reflects on the speech he has just delivered, he realizes that his role will demand that he do this regularly. In this moment, he finally understands what he has to do as a leader. And what is captured beautifully in this scene is that at his point of realization, his whole demeanor changes. He now projects a different energy and sense of confidence. When he takes a moment to thank his speech therapist, Lionel Logue, for his help. It is at this moment that Logue bows and addresses him as "Your Majesty" for the very first time.

Once King George gained the clarity he needed as a leader, commitment naturally followed, which in turn gave him the personal confidence to be a leader. The king of England truly became the king of England. Again, it was a visceral change. He knew it, and so did everyone else.

"This Is My Class!"

As I reflect over my own leadership career, I also knew when I had to make a leadership decision. Those moments always had a sense of clarity that led to a deep-seated sense of commitment. I knew exactly what needed to happen, what I had to do, and what I had to have my team do. I felt I was uniquely positioned to lead the way forward. However, this is not to imply that what I had to do was easy or that I never felt uncertainty or a sense of insecurity. Like all leaders, I had some tough situations to deal with. But when you fully decide, you know what's ahead and are prepared to do whatever you need to help your company, your team, and your customers succeed. That's the power of a leadership decision.

What I've also learned is you are not the only one making a decision. Your followers do as well. When you have clarity and commitment to your leadership decision, your followers will feel it. And if your decision is made for the right reasons, they will follow you. They will decide as well.

I experienced this early in my career. Soon after I left my first job, I started my own consulting business. I began doing more speaking and facilitation work, and I wanted to learn how to be very good at these tasks. I was able to work with a leading global leadership development company that was known for having an intense and excellent approach to developing speakers and facil-itators. I was accepted into the development program, and after many months of training, I needed to complete the last part of my development, which required me to teach two full courses with an experienced facilitator.

For my very first course, I was paired up with Don, a senior executive at the company and one of its most successful and popular leadership facilitators. He was one of the best that I've ever seen in action. Don was smart, funny, and had charisma with a great executive presence.

And then there was me: young and inexperienced but full of good intentions. I was thrilled and scared at the same time. As we began our program and our first class together, I could sense the participants forming an immediate bond with Don. They knew the deal. He was there to coach me and guide my development. The participants were kind to me, like people are kind to a sick animal or someone less fortunate. It was probably my own insecurities, but I could feel the climate in the room change when Don was up in the front working his magic, compared with when I was up front fumbling my way through the material. This went on for three weeks and then something happened. The company went through a shake-up, and Don was no longer an executive with the organization. He was, however, allowed to continue to work as a facilitator and program leader.

When I arrived at the next class after all this happened, Don was obviously not a happy man. His frustration was visible. He did not have a good night. His negativity influenced his facilitation. After the class, word got out about what had happened and the participants sympathized with him. Week five came, and it was more of the same. But now I could feel the class starting to get irritated with Don. Although I was progressing, I still had a long way to go to get to Don's level of mastery. Then at week six something happened. Don was really in the dumps, fairly disengaged, and essentially going through the motions. The class was now becoming disappointed in and less supportive of Don.

Halfway through that evening's program, the mood of the class was at an all-time low. No one was participating. We were only halfway through the program, and I knew that if Don didn't turn it around, the participants would stop showing up and demand their money back.

At that moment I realized what I had to do. I could feel it in my gut and in every cell of my body. I needed to be the leader of this class. I said to myself, "This is my class!" Once I declared this in my own mind, I found that I immediately relaxed. The nervousness and insecurity that I typically felt was now replaced with confidence.

I'm sure the class felt it, too. I became the leader, and they could look to me for the remaining six weeks of the program. And the participants responded. I could tell they were beginning to see me as the course leader.

Don and I never formally mentioned anything to the class. I made the leadership decision and changed the way I showed up. Don noticed and let me take over. In the end, the course was a huge success. The participants appreciated the experience. Don also thanked me for helping him through the last six weeks of the program. In fact, by the tenth class, he got his groove back and we worked together as co-facilitators and as peers.

Deciding Not to Lead Is an Important Leadership Decision

People often ask me, "What if you decide *not* to be a leader?" I believe this is also an important leadership decision to make. Big D leadership decisions are important because what you do as a leader matters. But if you make those decisions lightly, if you feel pressured to take on those roles, if you do it only for the money or the perks, then you run the risk of becoming an empty chair leader. You can fake it for a while, but eventually your lack of clarity and commitment will start to show. So the question comes back to you: Do you know yourself well enough to decide whether leadership is for you? Do you have the maturity and courage to say no? I believe we need more people to have the kind of self-awareness and personal maturity needed to make good leadership decisions, including the decision to turn down a role that is not right.

Steve Wozniak had the courage to say no. Long before he appeared on reality TV, Wozniak was the engineer who invented the first Apple computer. He was a programmer at HP when he was approached about the job at Apple. He knew he didn't want to be a corporate leader, so he was worried about joining a new company. But Apple promised him that he wouldn't have to go into management—he could stay at the bottom of the organization chart as an engineer. Apple turned to Mike Markkula, a successful angel investor, to run the company, and they let Wozniak keep doing what he did best. Although Wozniak didn't have the title, he was still an important technical leader in the company.

The Steve Wozniak story demonstrates the self-awareness that is necessary to make a leadership decision. Wozniak knew how he was wired, what he liked and didn't like to do, and where he could add value.

Keep in mind that your leadership decision can change. I was working with a client named Barb, the chief human resources officer of a global energy company. One day we were talking about some high-potential leaders in her company. She shared a story about one of her direct reports, Marcela.

In their development discussions, Marcela said to Barb, "I have been observing you in your role. I have seen you interact with our chief executive officer, other senior executives, board members, and the unions, and I can see how much pressure you are under. You know, I don't think I'm ready for this right now."

This is a great example of the work leaders need to do to gain personal clarity. Barb picked Marcela out as a hi-po, but Marcela didn't just stop there. She studied the demands of the role she was being groomed for, and she had enough self-awareness to know that she wasn't ready for it. That takes maturity and humility. Every organization needs more leaders like Marcela.

Marcela then spent the year reflecting on what she wanted to do. Like a great leader, Barb continued exposing Marcela to broader opportunities that gave her more information and insight. Then after 12 months, Marcela decided she was now ready. She had both the clarity and the commitment required to become a great leader. Barb was also confident that Marcela was ready for the right reasons.

Unfortunately, not everybody is as mature as Marcela, and not everyone has a boss like Barb. I've worked with plenty of leaders who have wanted to take on senior roles so desperately that they jump at the chance, not really understanding the demands of the role, only to falter months later. You must be self-aware enough to know whether you are ready. You also need to have the maturity to make this decision. You have to take this decision seriously—it's your responsibility to your organization and ultimately to yourself.

Final Thoughts—Get Your Act Together

All the great leaders I work with describe times when they made the conscious decision to be the leader. They relate experiences and situations that forced them to pause and think differently about who they are as leaders and what they are expected to do in their roles. These are the leaders who always seem to have their act together. It is pretty obvious that they are deliberate about the Big D leadership decisions they have to make. They also pay a lot of attention to the small d leadership decisions because they know just how important they can be, too. Whether you are making Big D or small d leadership decisions, you need two things: clarity and commitment. You need to be clear about what you are deciding, and once you have decided, you need to be committed to being the best leader you can be. And when you do that, you are fulfilling the first term of the leadership contract.

Reflect—Leadership Is a Decision

As you reflect on the ideas in this chapter, think about your answers to the following questions:

1. Have you ever jumped into a leadership opportunity without really appreciating what you were getting into? What were the implications? What do you know now about the role that you wished you knew when you first took it on?
2. What are the major complexities of your role?
3. Who is legitimately scrutinizing you? How are you handling it?
4. What are your leadership accountabilities?
5. How are you showing up as a leader? How are you getting in your own way of success?
6. What impact are you having? What value are you truly bringing as a leader?
7. When have you been in a situation that forced you to make the Big D leadership decision?
8. Think about the small d leadership decisions you find yourself in. What guides you when making these small d decisions?

CHAPTER 5

Leadership Is an Obligation—Step Up

In 1907, an American engineer named Theodore Cooper was leading a project to build the Québec Bridge, spanning the St. Lawrence River. Once complete, it would be one of the largest and longest structures ever built. It would provide an economic boost to the region, enabling goods to be shipped more easily by rail between the American New England states and the Canadian province of Québec.

Cooper was chosen because of his stellar reputation, illustrious career, and expertise in bridge building. His 1884 book, *General Specifications for Iron Railroad Bridges and Viaducts*, was the definitive textbook for other bridge design engineers at the time.

But on a hot summer's day in late August of that year, tragedy struck. Near the end of the workday, a worker was driving rivets into the southern span of the bridge. He noticed that the rivets he had driven in an hour before had snapped in two. As he was about to report his concerns to his foreman, the air was suddenly filled with the deafening sound of grinding metal.

The worker looked up and saw the bridge begin to fall into the water, creating a force like nothing he had ever felt before. The sound carried for miles. People in nearby Québec City felt an earthquakelike tremor.

Most of the 85 men working on the bridge were immediately catapulted hundreds of feet into the air as the bridge fell beneath their feet. They died the second they hit the water. Other workers were crushed or dragged underwater by the falling bridge. Some died onshore because rescuers couldn't free them from the twisted metal debris before the tide came in that night. The community watched helplessly as these workers drowned. Seventy-five men lost their lives that day.

A Royal Commission investigating the tragic event found that the bridge had collapsed under its own weight. Design errors and miscalculations of the load that the structure could bear were the root of the problem. But the issues went far beyond technical errors. The commission criticized Cooper and the bridge company for putting profit before the safety of the public.

Cooper came under fire because, although he was an expert in bridge design, he had never personally designed a bridge as large as the Québec Bridge. The commission also concluded that political and economic pressure had influenced his judgment. Finally, Cooper's arrogance kept him from heeding the many warning signs regarding the weight of the bridge and the quality of the materials that emerged during the construction. As author Kim Wedel chronicles in the book *The Obligation: A History of the Order of the Engineer*, "he had ignored too many warnings, shrugged off too many doubts, and as investment mounted and construction advanced, it only grew harder and harder for him to contemplate his errors. Perhaps by the time the massive project fell, he had decided it could not fall because he had designed it." Cooper's reputation collapsed when the bridge did.

It would take a full two years for all the metal debris to be cleared from the river. But even then the story of the Québec Bridge wasn't over. In 1916, a second attempt at building the bridge ended in another collapse. Thirteen more lives were lost. The two tragedies clearly showed that the engineering profession needed to change.

In 1918, reforms put the profession on a stronger foundation. Professional engineers would have to be licensed, and designs for public infrastructure projects would need to be approved by a licensed engineer. Then in 1925, a group of Canadian engineers established a ceremony called the Ritual of the Calling of an Engineer. They aimed to make graduating engineers aware of the obligations of their profession.

The Iron Ring Ceremony

Since that time, this ritual, now known as the Iron Ring Ceremony, has been conducted in universities across Canada. The secret ceremony highlights the obligations that engineers accept as they enter the profession. Older engineers retell the story of the Québec Bridge disaster so that the new graduates understand what can happen when their work is not done properly.

An iron ring is placed on the little finger of the dominant hand to act as a symbol and a reminder of the obligations that come from being an engineer. Since engineers wear the ring on their dominant hand, it rubs against every design they create, a constant reminder of their obligation to public safety and to the strong moral tenets that characterize professional engineers.

The design of the iron ring is also symbolic. New rings are made with rough edges to symbolize that a young engineer is rough and inexperienced. This instills a personal sense of humility and acts as a reminder of how much the engineer still has to learn. Over time, the rough edges begin to smooth out as the engineer creates design plans and gains experience, age, and wisdom. The ring is given to the young engineer by an older professional who will mentor the candidate.

During the ceremony, young engineers are also reminded never to lose their moral center in the face of external pressures. They must understand that what they do has a broader impact on the public. They are reminded that they will need to make ethical choices during their careers, and when they do so, they must not simply try to stay out of trouble; they must make decisions from a desire to maintain the highest possible standard for the engineering profession. The ceremony also stresses the need for a sense of camaraderie among professional engineers to support one another's development and growth.

In 1970, engineers in the United States began observing a similar ceremony called the Order of the Engineer. Building on the idea of the Iron Ring Ceremony, the order was intended to foster a spirit of pride and responsibility in the engineering profession, to bridge the gap between training and experience, and to present to the public a visible symbol identifying the engineer.

Over my career, I have worked with a lot of technical organizations and engineers. I truly respect and admire the care and concern engineers have for safety in the work that they do. They seem to carry the weight of their obligations front and center in their minds every single day.

I believe too many leaders today lack this sense of obligation. When people first take on leadership roles, nobody teaches them that leadership is an obligation. Look at the leaders at the center of scandals and corporate corruption. It's clear that many leaders have lost their way. They have either forgotten or were never aware of the obligations that come with being a leader.

This is why obligation is the second term of the leadership contract. As a leader, you need to step up and recognize that when you take on a leadership role, it's not all about you.

The ideas in this chapter may feel heavy to you. They should. As a leader, you need to feel the weight of your leadership obligations. If you don't, you run the risk of not living up to them, and we have seen what happens then. The consequences will go beyond you and end up affecting your customers, your organization, your employees, and your communities.

Assuming that you have truly decided to be a leader (the first point in the leadership contract), the next thing you need to realize is that I'm sure you have worked with leaders who were driven primarily by personal gain. For them, their leadership role was all about the money, the titles, the stock options, the company cars, the perks, and the power. Working with them, you got a sense that they missed something along the way. They just did not get it, or maybe they lost their way.

I work with a lot of executive teams for two- or three-day off-sites to discuss strategy and the future leadership of their organization, and I can always tell how the leaders are truly wired by what they talk about during their dinners together. Some teams continue the discussion from the day's meeting. Others talk about their personal lives. And then from time to time, you get the team that talks only about what's in it for them; hours of discussion follow about who is getting a new BMW or Audi as their company car or what other perks being handed out. I believe these leaders are missing the mark. I'm sure if their employees could hear these conversations, they would be very disappointed.

I believe this partly explains why there is such a low level of trust and confidence in senior leadership. Employees look to the upper echelons of their organizations and see leaders primarily motivated by personal gain. I suspect that if you asked, employees would say, "I see what's in it for you, but I don't see what's in it for the rest of us."

This is where we need to begin our reflection on the obligations of leadership. If you make it all about you, you won't be truly successful because you will be leading for the wrong reasons. You will be letting down everyone who is counting on you. More important, your true colors will shine through when your leadership is really tested.

Let's look at a couple of examples. I ask, however, that as you read these stories, you aren't too judgmental. Rather, you should learn from them. Put yourself in the shoes of the leader in the story. What would you have done in that person's situation? How would you have acted to resolve the crisis? In the end, this exericse is not about these leaders; it's about you and your leadership.

The Phone Hacking Scandal at News of the World

"Our reputation is more important than the last $100 million." These words are attributed to Rupert Murdoch. Unfortunately, his reputation and that of his company, News Corporation, were severely damaged when the world learned that reporters for the *News of the World* tabloid, one of Murdoch's publications, illegally accessed messages from the mobile phones of celebrities, politicians, and others. This was all done with the knowledge of the company's senior staff.

The scandal prompted Scotland Yard investigations, government inquiries, and the shutdown of the 168-year-old publication.

Rupert Murdoch was at the center of the story.[1] He blamed lower-ranking executives, saying they kept him in the dark about what was happening at the paper. Members of Parliament rejected this defense. They made some stinging statements in one of their reports[2]:

> *On the basis of the facts and evidence before the Committee, we conclude that, if at all relevant times Rupert Murdoch did not take steps to become fully informed about phone-hacking, he turned a blind eye and exhibited willful blindness to what was going on in his companies and publications. This culture, we consider, permeated from the top throughout the organization and speaks volumes about the lack of effective corporate governance at News Corporation and News International. We conclude, therefore, that Rupert Murdoch is not a fit person to exercise the stewardship of a major international company.*

The words *willful blindness* to me get to the heart of the way Murdoch failed to demonstrate his obligations as a leader. It's something that all leaders need to pay attention to in our own roles. It's easy to sit back and judge. It's harder to reflect on this example and apply it to our own leadership positions.

The phone hacking scandal tested Murdoch's leadership. In this moment of crisis he was criticized for blaming others and his "willful blindness" undermined his leadership. In the end, he was declared unfit to lead his company. And although there was plenty of media attention focused on Murdoch and the senior executives, little attention was paid to those affected by the scandal. Before the decision was made to close the *News of the World*, it was the most popular newspaper in Britain. The closure resulted in 200 employees losing their jobs, not to mention freelance writers and other contract employees. Understandably, the reaction from employees was shock, anger, and outrage. When leaders don't live up to their leadership obligations, innocent victims pay the price.

Take a moment to reflect on Murdoch's story. What insights from it do you gain as a leader?

British Petroleum (BP) Oil Rig Explosion in the Gulf of Mexico

On April 20, 2010, an explosion took place at the BP-contracted oil rig Deepwater Horizon, resulting in 11 deaths and 15 injuries. Three months later, after several failed attempts, the gushing wellhead was finally capped. Unfortunately, by that time, an estimated 4.9 million barrels of crude oil had been released in the Gulf of Mexico, causing extensive environmental damage.

Like News Corporation's phone hacking scandal, this crisis was a reputational nightmare for BP. Chief executive officer (CEO) Tony Hayward was in the spotlight, and he appeared to struggle with managing the situation right from the beginning. His credibility steadily eroded from the first day of the crisis to the time he finally stepped down from his role as CEO. During that time he made a series of statements that made him seem out of touch with the situation and its impact on the people and the area.

Just after the explosion, Hayward was said to have asked his executive team, "What the hell did we do to deserve this?" This created the impression that he was more concerned with himself in that moment than with people much more deeply affected by the explosion. Then on May 30, 2010, in a TV interview, Hayward expressed remorse for the massive disruption the spill had caused to the lives of people living in the area. Then he said, "There's no one who wants this thing over more than I do. I'd like my life back."

And with those words he was done. His story spread through the media and seemed to be the final nail in his coffin. His credibility and that of BP was destroyed. In making that statement, however sincere he may have been, he once again created the impression that in that moment of crisis he was thinking of himself and not of the environment or the communities and citizens affected. His words made it appear as if it were all about him. Maybe that was never his intent. Maybe in a moment of weakness his words didn't come out as he intended. However, those words did generate a reaction. How was the public expected to feel sorry for him when millions of barrels of crude oil had caused environmental damage in the region and thousands upon thousands of lives were affected?

Both Murdoch's and Hayward's stories are strong examples of the challenges in leadership today. They show what a high degree of scrutiny looks like and what all leaders face in times like this. It may be easy to stand back and judge, but these stories point to the fact that when any bad decision, misstep, or public slipup all of a sudden hits the media, everything you've worked so hard to build begins to crumble. Welcome to the realities of leadership today.

This is why it's important for you to really appreciate that regardless of the industry you work in or the level of leadership role you have, you need to understand that leadership is an obligation. But in the past 30 years there have been far too many crises that have made the public question whether leaders truly understand their obligations.

Union Carbide's Toxic Gas Leak in India

Take, for example, Union Carbide's toxic gas leak in Bhopal, India, which occurred on December 3, 1984, in a pesticide plant operated by an Indian subsidiary.[3] An estimated 40 tons of methyl isocyanate gas leaked from the plant, immediately killing at least 3,800 people and causing significant morbidity and premature death for many thousands more. In addition, more than half a million others reported health problems. The company came under fire for the way it handled the situation. Its first reaction was to disassociate itself from any legal responsibility. It also attempted to shift blame to the local company because it was a subsidiary plant. Finally it created scenarios claiming the plant was sabotaged by extremist groups and disgruntled employees. In the end, none of this mattered, as the company's reputation was harmed beyond repair. It eventually paid $470 million in compensation, which many believe was a relatively small amount based on the leak's significant environmental and health impacts. Union Carbide was eventually sold to Dow Chemical Co.

Consider also the experience of the Exxon Valdez oil spill that spewed 11 million gallons of crude into Alaska's Prince William Sound, killing hundreds of thousands of birds and marine animals. The company and its leaders also came under fire for appearing aloof, deflecting blame, and not taking full responsibility for the events.

Sadly, these aren't the only examples of failed leadership. Think of WorldCom, Enron, Arthur Andersen, Tyco, Citicorp, AIG, Lehman Brothers—the list goes on and on. There are far too many examples of leaders failing to live up to the obligations of leadership.

What is most startling to me is that in the past 30 years there appears to be only one real example of an organization whose leaders lived up to their obligations in times of crisis: Johnson & Johnson. It's a story that has been told and retold time and time again in leadership books and in MBA courses. I can't help but ask myself: Is this the only really good example we have in over 30 years? Does that paucity of such stories in fact tell us something?

In 1982, seven people in the Chicago area died after taking Tylenol. Someone had laced the pills with potassium cyanide. Johnson & Johnson immediately accepted responsibility and pulled every bottle off store shelves. In the end, the company's leaders relied on the Johnson & Johnson Credo, which always puts the welfare of the public and health care professionals above company profits. Johnson & Johnson leaders should be applauded for their efforts, but the rest of us should be embarrassed by the fact that this is one of the very few positive examples of leaders living up to their obligations in recent history.

What's It Going to Take?

So the question I'm left with is this: What's it going to take for leaders to truly understand the obligations of leadership? Harvard Professor Barbara Kellerman[4] says that leaders today need to be held accountable for their actions and bad behavior just like other professionals in health care or law. When their actions or negligence cause harm, she argues, leaders should be sued for "leadership malpractice." She cites the many CEOs who leave companies after years of poor performance without suffering any consequence, departing with generous packages ensuring their own financial security even though they failed to protect employees and stockholders. Leadership needs to be considered its own profession. Medical doctors, lawyers, and engineers have professional standards. Leadership needs an established set of standards, too.

Although the idea for a set of standards has merit, I believe we need to start with something more fundamental. We need to be more explicit in helping leaders understand what their obligations of leadership are and what they must do to live up to them. Take a moment to reflect on your own leadership experience. Think about the first time you took on a leadership role? Did you ever really stop to think about the obligations you were assuming as you took on that role? I would go further and suggest that your boss or organization probably didn't sit you down to say, "Listen, here's what your obligations are as a leader." I'm sure that rarely happens. If you are like most leaders I work with, you probably had to figure it out on your own. Now, most leaders are pretty smart people, and eventually, they might get it on their own. But what if they never do? I don't believe we can just rely on happenstance. We need to be more deliberate and get clear on our obligations as leaders.

I'll also let you in on a secret so that you don't have to figure it out all on your own: In order to be effective, sometimes you will need to separate your personal feelings about your obligations as a leader. Let me explain. You need an ability to separate your personal opinions from your professional obligations. It takes a strong person to be able to have this level of personal insight, but it's going to be crucial to your success as a leader, especially as you move into more senior-level roles.

A great example of this inner conflict comes from a *West Wing* episode. Jed Bartlet, played by Martin Sheen, is the president of the United States. He's dealing with one of his biggest dilemmas as president. There is an inmate on death row, and Bartlet is under great pressure to intervene and give a stay of execution. He reaches out to many people to get advice. He asks an old personal friend—a priest, played by Karl Malden—to visit him. When the priest arrives, he is in awe of the Oval Office. After some small chitchat, the priest asks President Bartlet, "How do you want me to call you, Jed or Mr. President?" The president pauses and replies, "Mr. President." He feels compelled to explain his reasons. He insists that it is not about ego. Instead, as a president he has to make very important decisions: which disease gets funding or which troops are sent into battle. He continues by saying that when confronted with these kinds of decisions, it is important for him to think of the office, rather than the man. It's a brilliant moment in the episode and a brilliant line. It demonstrates a leader who never loses sight of his broader professional obligations. He realizes it's not about him; it's about the role he has and he needs a way to separate the man from the office so that he can effectively fulfill his obligations.

I have personally found this idea helpful in my own leadership role, not in such a dramatic way as in the previous example, but important nonetheless. I remember a shift I had in my own mind during one team meeting. We were debating a strategy we were working on. My team is filled with smart and passionate consultants who vigorously position their ideas. In this discussion, we were reaching a bit of an impasse. As I watched the discussion, I realized that I was pushing hard to get my own idea across. Then I stopped myself and asked, "What's my obligation right now as a leader?"

The answer immediately came to me. My obligation was not to sell my idea to the team. In fact, as the team leader I could have just dictated what I wanted, but I knew that wasn't what was best for our business. My obligation in that moment was to create the best possible conditions for my management team and me to think through our strategy. That was my obligation as the leader of the team. It was my obligation to my CEO, my board, and my clients and shareholders. This ability to be able to separate the person (what you are personally vested in) from your professional leadership obligations is critical for you to master. The first step begins with having clarity about the core obligations you must live up to as a leader. That's where we are going next.

The Five Core Obligations of Leadership

"Who is *the company*?" That's what one of my clients recently asked his colleagues. We were in the middle of a session on leadership, and this senior vice president was trying to explain his idea of what it means to be a leader. He said that when he first became a manager, he was thrilled to have the opportunity. He got completely wrapped up in the title, the extra money, and the power that his role provided. He finally felt like the big man on campus.

But the longer he stayed in the job, the more frustrated he became. As a manager, he now had a closer view of how the company operated than he had in his previous role. He could see bigger challenges and more serious dysfunctions than he had ever seen before. And he kept complaining, saying to himself, "This 'company' has got to get its act together!"

For a long time, he believed the company was a thing—an external entity that was separate from himself. He kept blaming the company's senior leaders for the problems he was experiencing.

Then he said, "When I took on this senior leadership role, I soon realized 'the company' wasn't a 'thing' at all—the company was me. I was the company." He said that at that moment he shifted his focus as a leader. "I soon learned that it wasn't all about me. I had to live up to higher expectations."

With that realization, he stopped being a self-centered manager and started being a real leader, one who was aware of his obligations to the success of the organization.

He stopped looking at his role through the lens of what was in it for him. He started to understand and accept the broader obligations of leadership—that a leader is someone who takes accountability for the company and its customers, its employees, and the communities in which it does business. He began to feel the weight of being a real leader and realized that a lot rested on him now. He developed a real commitment to his leadership role and the obligations it demanded.

All leaders have obligations. Some are legal, some financial, and some moral and social in nature. In the end, your obligations as a leader are about a sense of duty or a promise to those you work with and those affected by what you do. Your leadership obligations should compel you to lead for the common good.

There are five core obligations that all leaders must understand, internalize, and live up to. I will outline them next.

Your Obligation to Yourself

When you take on a leadership role for the right reasons, you should feel the weight of being a real leader—the realization that a lot is resting on you and that a lot is expected of you. You must realize that you have an obligation to yourself to be the best leader you can possibly be. When you understand that core obligation, you will find it actually feels good to live up to your potential, to grow, to not stagnate or become an empty chair leader.

Unfortunately, too many leaders fail to live up to even this first obligation. As Linda Hill and Kent Lineback, authors of the book *Being the Boss: The 3 Imperatives for Becoming a Great Leader*, explain, too many leaders stop working on themselves. They reach a level of performance and stop growing, assuming they are fully formed. They stop challenging themselves. As a result, many derail. Others fail to live up to their potential. In the end, they don't live up to their personal obligations—their commitment to being the best leader possible.

I work with leaders like this all the time. We come into their organizations to deliver leadership programs, and they assume the development opportunities are for other leaders, not for them. They think they are exempt because they don't believe they need the development.

But your obligations to yourself go even deeper. It demands that you have the self-awareness and honesty to understand where you may get yourself into trouble as a leader. Too many leaders assume leadership roles with arrogance instead of humility. When you start from a position of humility, you recognize that you work in a complex world. At any moment something can happen in your operating environment to test the capacity of your leadership.

You must also recognize that leadership brings temptations: power, money, greed, success, and fame. Many leaders who fail to live up to their personal obligations don't effectively manage these temptations. And there are other temptations to look out for as well: sex, alcohol, and drugs. We all have seen leaders ruined by scandals of all kinds. I have also seen many leaders who have undermined their own credibility and authority because they couldn't manage these temptations. Do you know what will tempt you as a leader?

Your obligations to yourself as a leader mean you need to strengthen your personal health through regular exercise, by building a strong family life and a personal support network, and by maintaining a sense of personal balance.

Ultimately your main obligation is simple: to be the leader. A few years back I was watching a segment on effective parenting on TV. Hidden cameras were installed in the home of a family with a typical mom, dad, and two of the most unruly teenagers you've ever seen. A week went by and the parent expert brought in by the program was working with the parents and showing them clips from the week. It was hard to watch. The teenagers demonstrated no respect for their parents. They argued continually with their parents, disputing every decision the parents tried to make. The parents joined in, arguing with their teens rather than disciplining them, and every encounter ended up in a shouting match. Then the parenting expert said to the parents as they were watching one of the worst arguments of the week, "Tell me, who are the parents in this situation?" The two parents were a little confused but then said, "We are." Then the parenting expert said, "Then why are you behaving just like your children?" He went on to explain that, as parents, they ultimately have an obligation to be the parents, no matter how tough it may be in the midst of the situation. He reminded them, "Be the parent."

I use a similar line with my own team, but I modify it a little to "Be the leader." No matter how tough or challenging a situation may be at work, no matter how difficult the conflict, as a leader you have the obligation to be the leader. That's what you need to live up to. That's the higher standard you are being held to. It's the pace you need to set.

A question I'm often asked is "Vince, this is easy when you have a great boss, but what if your boss is a jerk or is completely uninspiring?" I know this is difficult, but you must still keep to a higher standard of leadership. A client of mine shared a great quote with me about this issue: "Don't lead as you are led, but lead as you know you must." That's what sets the great leaders apart from the rest. They maintain their obligation as a leader even when surrounded by lame leadership.

What's the obligation you have to yourself as a leader?

Your Obligation to Your Customers

There's a line that I share with my team all time: "In our business, nothing happens until a customer decides to buy something." The reason that this is an important idea is that I find many leaders take their customers for granted. Sure, we talk a lot about being customer-focused or exceeding customer expectations, but the reality is that many leaders rarely lead with the obligation to the customers at the front of their minds. In fact, one of the telltale signs of this is when I work with new clients. I always pay attention to their language when they speak during meetings. It's surprising to me how often senior leaders can spend days talking about strategy, and yet the word *customer* never even surfaces.

Your obligation as a leader is to lead in a way that is focused on delivering value to your customers. That's the promise that every organization ultimately makes. As a leader, you need to be clear about your customers' needs and expectations. This will help you ensure that business decisions and priorities are focused on delivering value. You need to make sure their your organization's products and services are designed to meet or exceed your customers' expectations.

You have an obligation to treat your customers fairly. If you drop the ball in the course of doing business with them, you need to take accountability and respond quickly to make things better. You also need to act as their advocate in your own organization so that everyone inside understands the needs of your customers.

When you get your obligation to your customers right, you get their loyalty. But it doesn't last forever. The pressure is always on, and you can never forget your obligation to them. In my experience, I find there is one simple way to keep this obligation front and center in your mind as a leader, and it comes down to one word: *gratitude*.

When you are grateful for your customers, you recognize that your business wouldn't exist without them. I have talked to owner-operators of construction companies, retail stores, and other small businesses, and these self-employed individuals always seem to have a genuine sense of gratitude because they know their customers have plenty of choices when it comes to where to spend their money.

In our competitive world, customers have choices. And when they choose you and your organization, you need to be grateful. You need to make sure that this sense of gratitude is in the front of your mind when you work with them so that they actually feel it.

How would you define your obligation to your customers?

Your Obligation to Your Organization

Sam Palmisano, the former CEO of IBM, was asked in an interview about his key obligation as a leader. He saw his obligation as being a temporary steward of the enterprise. It wasn't about him and his own ego. Instead, he was clear that his core obligation was *to leave IBM stronger than when he took it over.* And in his 11 years as CEO, he did just that. For example, the company's return on capital increased from 4.7 percent when he first started his role to 15.1 percent when he left it. But he also balanced strong financial results, with an unrelenting focus on developing future leaders. Geoff Colvin of *Fortune* magazine wrote that Palmisano left a legacy of leadership at IBM,[5] and this is what made him a truly rare leader. How rare? Bill George from Harvard Business School defined him as the best CEO of the twenty-first century—an individual able to blend humility and openness with directness and pragmatism.[6]

Always focus on having a long-term view of success. This is a characteristic of strong leaders that I've witnessed over the years. They understand that the old model of heroic leaders is archaic. They see themselves as part of a community of peers. Not only are they clear on their obligations from a financial standpoint, but they understand their broader obligations to the health and sustainability of their organizations.

As a leader, you have a core obligation to ensure the future success and long-term sustainability of your organization—an obvious point. Unfortunately, I see too many leaders acting as bystanders in their organizations: standing around watching projects derail or seeing problems but not jumping in to fix them. Just going through the motions and thinking that it's someone else's responsibility is simply not good enough. Other leaders squander financial resources without thinking about the impact on the business. Many fail to actively manage poor performers, not realizing they are undermining the success of the organization. This also isn't good enough anymore.

If any of this is sounding familiar or sounding like you, it's time you start rethinking how you are leading.

I worked with an organization that had several distinct lines of business. One leader, Wayne, led a business that was doing well. However, there were early warning signs that his market was shifting in ways that could put his business at risk. But those warning signs seemed like they were in the far distance. He didn't need to pay attention to them because his business was doing so well in the present. But then growth began to stall. Before Wayne knew it, all those warning signs came together to disrupt his market in ways he never imagined. In executive meetings, he shared his surprise, claiming that these market forces emerged almost overnight. They didn't. Although he was meeting his obligation by driving short-term growth of his organization, he failed to pay attention to his long-term obligation to the success of his organization. By the time he realized he had to act, he had missed his chance.

You must step up to your obligation to your organization. You must roll up your sleeves to make things better every single day— in ways that position your organization for both short- and long-term success. That's the obligation you have taken on, whether you are aware of it or not. When you show up each day, you work in the interest of the whole enterprise. You don't focus only on your own department or functional area or your own self-interests. You need to anticipate threats in your operating environment that can put your organization at risk. You must create a sustainable business strategy that will drive competitive advantage over the long term.

You must build strong relationships with other stakeholders, such as suppliers, regulators, and unions. In too many organizations, these relationships are adversarial, strained, and unproductive. You must work to improve them in order to live up to your obligation to your organization.

In the end, I find that leaders who truly understand their obligation to their organization see it as a living thing, something that has to be cared for in order to ensure its long-term survival and success.

How would you define your obligation to your organization?

If you are a frontline leader, it might be as simple as ensuring the high performance of your team. If you are a mid-level leader, it may be to drive organizational-wide change. If you are an executive leader, it may be to ensure your company has a strong pipeline of future leaders or that you have a compelling strategy that will drive sustainable future growth.

Your Obligation to Your Employees

As a leader, you also have an obligation to your employees. This means committing to creating a positive leadership experience for them by establishing a compelling culture—a work environment based on respect and dignity that encourages a positive working relationship, celebrates success, and makes employees feel valued. It also means making tough but important decisions that will protect the health of your organization's culture.

When you create a compelling culture, your employees will be fully engaged and your customers will feel that engagement. I have learned that a positive leadership experience translates into a positive employee experience, which in turn creates a strong customer experience.

As a leader you also have an obligation to make sure your employees understand the company's strategy so that they understand how their work contributes to the overall success of your organization. This is what makes work meaningful.

Once you ensure that employees have clarity, you then must support them in their ability to get work done. This means you need to remove obstacles that impede their performance and you need to support their ongoing development and growth.

In the end you need to love helping people grow by challenging and stretching them. You can't own the success or engagement of your employees—they have their part to play. But you certainly do own creating the conditions for employees to thrive. You must pay attention to their own career development by having career discussions. Think of your own experiences when you've been at your best as an employee. Chances are you had a leader who took her obligation to her employees as seriously as every other obligation she had. She focused on your personal growth and career development.

Think of your current role and ask yourself: How am I living up to my obligation to my employees?

Your Obligation to Your Communities

Charles Garfield was a pioneering researcher in the area of personal and organizational peak performance. He recognized decades ago that we can't create successful organizations in the midst of a decaying society. He believed, and I agree with him, that organizations and the communities in which they do business are deeply connected.

Authors Jeffrey Gandz, Mary Crossan, Gerard Seijts, and Carol Stephenson, in the manifesto *Leadership on Trial*,[7] go even further, arguing that being responsible for personal and corporate actions is ultimately a moral obligation of leadership. They write, "To the extent that business benefits from what a society has to offer, it is morally obligated to contribute to the health and welfare of that society."

This means always making the ethical choice and considering the ethical dimension of every decision, even the small ones. It also means accepting the responsibility to clean up when mistakes happen and harm is done. Leaders do have an obligation to the communities in which they do business.

This obligation means you pay attention to the obvious things. You pay your taxes. You behave like a good corporate citizen. You take responsibility for the environment. You support local groups, schools, and charities. You understand that creating a successful organization is important to the communities in which you do business. Successful organizations create economic value. They create jobs. They become multipliers for a host of local businesses that depend on you. These ideas are not new, but it's time that we remind ourselves of them.

Michael Porter[8] says that companies must take the lead in bringing business and society back together. At the core is the idea of creating shared value, which is defined as policies and practices that enhance the competitive advantage of organizations while simultaneously advancing the economic and social conditions in the communities in which those organizations operate. I believe this concept will define a key obligation for future leaders. It's time to understand and internalize this obligation and move it from an idea into action.

The good news is that a growing number of organizations are attempting to redefine leadership and business in ways that enable them to do well by also doing good. The two are not mutually exclusive. John Mackey, co-CEO of Whole Foods Markets, is leading the way. In his book *Conscious Capitalism*,[9] he and his co-author Rajendra Sisodia state that business has to redefine its purpose beyond solely making money. They argue that for too long we have come to believe that the only purpose of a company is to make money. They say, however, that it's time to move beyond that single objective. The authors share an analogy. A human body needs to make red blood cells to live but the purpose of life and the purpose of a human body aren't solely to produce red bloods cells. A higher and broader purpose exists. It's time for businesses and corporations to find that broader purpose, contributing to society and making the world a better place.

The challenge we have is that a lot of the work done in the area of corporate, environmental, or social responsibility makes this obligation feel like an abstract goal. I was working with a client's top 30 high-potential leaders. They were seen as potential successors to the company's executive-level roles. One of the senior vice presidents was brought into a session to provide a presentation on the company's corporate social responsibility (CSR) strategy. As she went through her slides, I could see the ideas were falling flat. In the end, the CSR strategy was seen as just another corporate initiative, with clever branding and messaging. The real message was lost on those leaders.

As a leader today you need to come to terms with how you will live up to this important obligation. We can no longer pay lip service to our CSR. We need to evolve our thinking as leaders to create shared value and find a broader purpose for our organizations. The good news is there is no better time for companies to do well by doing good. It's a powerful legacy we can all leave as leaders.

The Five Core Obligations in Action

Let's examine a story of a leader and his organization and how he stepped up to the five core obligations in a time of crisis.

The Listeria *Bacteria Outbreak at Maple Leaf Foods*

Maple Leaf Foods is a leading consumer packaged food company with operations across the United Kingdom, North America, and Asia. In the summer of 2008, one of the company's Canadian plants had an outbreak of the *Listeria* bacteria in some of its packaged meat products. Nine deaths were caused by the tainted meat. Another 11 deaths were later linked to it. Hundreds of others became violently ill after eating the products.

The company's CEO, Michael McCain, was at the center of the story. He was the face of the company through the crisis, and he immediately issued an apology and accepted responsibility for the tainted meat. The company quickly recalled more than 200 brands of meat and tens of thousands of individual packages that were manufactured or packaged in the plant. McCain went on television and YouTube to make a public apology. He was genuine, obviously distraught by what had happened, and clear about the company's responsibility and accountability for what the outbreak. McCain talked about how he personally took this situation into his own hands.

> *Going through the crisis there are two advisors I've paid no attention to. The first are the lawyers, and the second are the accountants. It's not about money or legal liability; this is about our being accountable for providing consumers with safe food. This is a terrible tragedy. To those people who have become ill, and to the families who have lost loved ones, I want to express my deepest and most sincere sympathies. Words cannot begin to express our sadness for your pain.*

The company created a new role, chief safety officer. To mark the one-year anniversary of the outbreak, Maple Leaf Foods published a letter from the CEO in all the major newspapers. The letter said the company was committed to becoming a global leader in food safety in order to prevent this kind of tragedy from ever happening again: "On behalf of our 24,000 employees, we promise to never forget."

How did McCain and his company live up to the obligations of leadership? They didn't dodge responsibility. They didn't try to divert blame or avoid litigation. They took complete responsibility, due in part to a set of personal values on the part of the CEO, and a clear sense of obligation to customers, employees, and the broader communities in which Maple Leaf does business. This story stands out because it is so different from what we typically see during times of crisis. There are lessons here for all leaders to consider.

Revisiting the Iron Ring Ceremony and What It Means for Leaders

I believe that we as leaders need a version of the Iron Ring Ceremony to help us understand our leadership obligations.

What I especially like about the Iron Ring Ceremony is that it instills early on the ideas of humility, obligation, and deliberateness. At the core of the ceremony—and the meaning behind the symbolic iron ring—is the idea that engineers must be humble. They understand that what they do has a broader impact on the public and society as a whole. They are told that like the ring, they are rough and inexperienced and must grow and develop over time. And they are promised that they'll be supported by a mentor.

Let's contrast this experience to what happens to most new leaders. First, there isn't a ceremony like the Iron Ring Ceremony that helps you understand the obligations of leadership. Second, if you're lucky, you may get a mentor or a coach to help you integrate in your first 100 days, but for most people the experience of leadership is pretty isolating. There is little support and guidance. You feel like you've been thrown in the deep end of a pool, and you must sink or swim. Finally, and more important, most people who take on leadership roles do it with a sense of bravado and arrogance instead of humility. You feel like you can't admit that you have rough edges because you can't show your weaknesses or vulnerabilities. You also feel intense pressure to prove yourself at all costs. Maybe this is why up to 40 percent of leaders fail after assuming new leadership roles.

Rosabeth Moss Kanter from Harvard Business School[10] says that leaders today need a healthy dose of humility. They need a deep desire to serve others, with an emphasis on values and a sense of purpose, a sense of the long-term consequences of one's actions, and personal knowledge of one's strengths and limitations. Ultimately, she says that as a leader you must have a desire to do what's right for the common good, not just what's good for you.

Final Thoughts—Leadership Is an Obligation

It's also important to understand that living up to each of the five obligations of leadership isn't easy. At times they will be in conflict with one another. Inherent tensions will arise that you need to manage. Trade-offs will have to be made. In these cases, you need to recognize there will be no easy or trite answer that will resolve things for you. Leadership is never that easy, as much as we might want it to be. If you are truly aware, however, of what your obligations as a leader are and never lose sight of them while you lead, you will be better able to manage the inherent tensions that will arise. It's not enough that only you are aware of your core obligations at a personal level; every leader in your organization must do the same. When we do this, we can start a dialogue where the obligations become clearer and more transparent. We become more aware of what we truly believe in and what we may merely be paying lip service to. In the end, this process helps all leaders step up.

Reflect—Leadership Is an Obligation

As you reflect on the ideas in this chapter, think about your answers to the following questions:

1. What do you define as your primary obligation as a leader?
2. To what extent do you lead every day with this obligation front and center in your mind?

3. Consider the five core obligations of leadership described in this chapter. What insights did you gain regarding your obligation to:
   a. Yourself as a leader?
   b. Your customers?
   c. Your organization?
   d. Your employees?
   e. The communities in which your organization does business?
4. Would you say that you are living up to the five core obligations of leadership?
5. What actions will you take to live up to your core obligations as a leader?
6. Where do you need to really challenge yourself?

CHAPTER 6

Leadership Is Hard Work—Get Tough

et's face it: Leadership is hard work, and it's getting harder. To truly excel, to truly be a great leader over the long term, you must have the courage and persistence to do the hard work of leadership. Delivering consistent financial results, attaining high team performance, executing strategy, managing multiple and often conflicting priorities, and driving innovation isn't easy. You must realize that there is hard work that you alone as a leader can and must do, and if you don't do it, you'll set yourself and your organization back.

However, in my experience I find many leaders who are reluctant to dig in and choose instead to avoid the hard work. Others act as bystanders, watching things happen. And then there are those leaders who simply look for the easy way out, thinking that some quick-fix idea will make everything better, only to be surprised when these quick fixes don't fix anything. We need to stop underestimating what it takes to be a consistently great leader. Sure, leadership can be easy if you're satisfied with mediocrity. But that's not what the leadership contract is all about.

It's time that we as leaders understand that the real work of leadership isn't easy. We also need to understand that we'll need resilience, determination, and a deep sense of personal resolve to be effective. This is what the third term of the leadership contract is all about.

Do We Have Wimps or Leaders in Our Organizations?

A lot of my clients talk about how their leaders don't seem to be willing to take on the hard work that comes with their roles. I often hear comments like "Our leaders avoid managing poor performers," "Our leaders don't give candid feedback," or "Our leaders really struggle in making difficult decisions."

Hearing the same themes over and over again, from client after client, I can't help but ask myself, *Are there any real leaders in our organizations, or are we just surrounded by wimps?* It seems like there are a lot of wimps out there—people who don't have the courage to take on the hard work of leadership.

Holding people accountable isn't easy. Managing poor performers isn't easy. Accepting candid feedback about how you need to grow as a leader isn't easy. Confronting your personal gaps takes courage. But instead of getting tough, too many leaders choose to wimp out.

You must accept this third term of the leadership contract. You can't take the easy way out. It's no longer good enough for you to be a bystander. You have to get tough. Everyone, including your team, your department, your boss, and your organization, is counting on you to be a leader and not wimp out. This will also mean you will need to be tough with yourself.

The Hard Rule of Leadership

If you are ready to be a true leader, then it's time to learn a rule that few leaders understand. I call it the hard rule of leadership:

If you avoid the hard work of leadership, you will become a weak leader. If you tackle the hard work of leadership, you'll become a strong leader.

Let's explore this further.

Avoid the Hard Work of Leadership and You Become Weak

Take a moment to be honest with yourself and think about the hard rule of leadership as it applies to you. What hard work are you avoiding in your role? Maybe there's a difficult decision that you alone need to make. Maybe there's some straight-up feedback you need to deliver to a colleague. Maybe there's a chronic underperformer you know you need to deal with but haven't. Maybe you've been putting off doing a 360-degree assessment on yourself for fear of the feedback you'll receive.

Many leaders don't realize that when you avoid the hard work of leadership you actually end up making yourself weak. And it goes beyond you. You also end up weakening your team, your division, and your entire organization. The hard work will always be there, and if you keep putting it off, you'll spend your days dealing with the same issues over and over again. You'll never truly advance or make progress. You, your team, and your organization will be stuck. Does this sound familiar?

Let's consider the story of Margaret. She was a senior leader in a struggling information technology professional services firm. The company brought in a new chief operating officer, and he engaged me to help him and his senior team create a new strategy for the future. We set up regular forums for the top leaders to come together, and Margaret was one of those leaders. By the third session, I noticed Margaret was really getting frustrated.

I said, "Margaret, what's going on? You don't look like a happy camper."

She paused and then said in frustration, "I'm getting sick and tired of these meetings. You know I've come to all of them with this list of things I need to get done, and every time I walk away, my list remains untouched."

I said, "Okay, Margaret, thanks for sharing your reactions. Why don't you take a minute and review this list right now and ask yourself how many items could have been tackled before coming to this meeting?" As she was looking at her list, I said, "Margaret, I want you to be honest with me."

She looked up sheepishly, and said, "All of them."

I said, "What do you think has been holding you back?"

She paused and then explained, "Because they involve a lot of really tough conversations with the people in this room."

I reminded Margaret and the entire group that the purpose of the meetings was to explore the future strategy of the organization. They couldn't afford to get bogged down in day-to-day operational issues. It was their job as leaders to tackle those operational issues head-on, no matter how difficult they might be. I challenged the group to come to the meetings with as many items checked off their lists as possible so that they would have the freedom to think about the future. During the rest of the day, I saw Margaret meeting with her colleagues, booking times to address the hard things she was avoiding. It was clear she had learned the hard rule of leadership.

Many leaders don't understand that it is their job to get tough and tackle the hard stuff. Like Margaret, many never check a single thing off that list we all carry with us. Maybe confronting our peers is too difficult. Maybe it never seems like it's the right time to do it.

Unfortunately, a failure of nerve is a failure of leadership. Failing to have these conversations keeps you and your company from moving forward. It keeps you distracted by unresolved issues. It keeps you stuck.

The 10 Ways Leaders Make the Hard Work Harder

Through my own leadership experience and my work with hundreds of leaders at all levels, I've learned that not only is leadership hard work, but a lot of us inadvertently make the hard work harder. We need to be aware of how we do this so that we can become stronger as leaders.

As you read this next section, reflect on your own leadership roles and identify the ways you make the hard work of leadership even harder for yourself.

1. Getting in over Your Head   Sometimes a situation changes, and you're no longer equipped to manage it. Maybe you don't have the skills you need to be successful. Maybe your ego gets in the way and keeps you from asking for help. Maybe you are still trying to prove yourself to your colleagues and your organization. Maybe you lack self-confidence, and everyone knows it. Your team can smell it, and it undermines your credibility. You start playing it safe and become an empty chair leader. If this sounds familiar, you may be in over your head.

I once worked with a struggling leader whose performance began to decline. He was well liked, but pretty soon that didn't matter because his poor performance started to frustrate his team members. He knew he wasn't cut out for the role he was in. But instead of admitting it and addressing it directly, he let his performance slide to a point where his manager had to terminate him. If you find yourself in so far over your head that there's a real risk that your projects will have bad outcomes, then you need to have the courage to ask for help. Otherwise, you'll keep yourself and everyone around you stuck at the level of your incompetence.

We create risk for our organizations when we lack the courage to admit that we're in over our heads. Asking for help isn't easy. Your ego gets in the way. You probably feel tremendous pressure to prove yourself to others. But in today's complex world, you need to continually monitor your own performance and make sure you aren't putting yourself and your company at risk.

Do you find yourself getting in over your head as a leader?

2. Confusing Tough with Rough There aren't many really tough leaders out there. There are a lot of leaders who think they are *tough*, but they're actually *rough*. They've confused the two. They're holding on to old ideas of leadership that tell them you need to be a jerk to show how tough you are. Many of these leaders regularly mistreat, disrespect, and insult others. They frequently "tear a strip" off their direct reports, even in public. Yelling at people is easy. Being genuinely tough is much harder.

If you are one of these rough leaders who is prone to temper tantrums, emotional outbursts, or chronic moodiness, I have two words for you: Grow up! This behavior is understandable for tod-dlers but not for leaders. Your lack of professional maturity makes things harder for you. Your inability to keep your emotions in check puts everyone on edge. You're creating a climate of fear, and you'll never get the best out of your team and colleagues as a result.

A generation ago it was probably okay to mistreat people. Leaders could do it because they had power and the boomers would put up with it. But if you take the rough approach today, you'll become a lonely leader pretty fast. The bottom line is that if you are a jerk as a leader, no one is going to want to work with you. It's that simple. Why? Because the Millennials won't put up with you; they'll just leave. To make matters worse, the boomers are following their younger col-leagues' lead and becoming less willing to put up with a rough leader.

As a leader do you confuse tough with rough?

3. Mistaking Effort for Results   Vic was pretty angry when he left his annual performance review. He couldn't believe his boss, the company's chief information officer (CIO), had given him an unsatisfactory performance rating. Didn't she know how hard he had been working?

As the director of IT, Vic's big project for the year was implementing a new cloud-based customer relationship manage-ment (CRM) system. He had run into problems right from the start. The first vendor he chose wasn't really up to the task. They gave him bad advice, and by the time he realized it, months had gone by and the project's costs had escalated. Now he was under pressure to get the system out, so he skimped on internal educa-tion. When the CRM hit the sales force, he got a lot of complaints.

Vic thought he had given the project everything he could. It had been a hard year. He had put in countless hours. He was often on call 24/7. And he felt like hiccups were common enough anyway when implementing a new system to not be a big concern.

His manager saw things differently. She knew how many hours Vic had put in, but in the end, he just didn't deliver. So although

Vic rated himself as "meeting expectations" for the year, his manager gave him that dreaded rating of "unsatisfactory."

During the meeting, the CIO explained that, as a leader, Vic shouldn't confuse effort with results. "It's one of the first ground rules of leadership," she said. She also reminded him that as a leader, he needed to be able to take an objective view of his own performance, even when it fell short.

I've run into leaders like Vic many times. They're so focused on how hard they're working that they can't see the actual results they've accomplished—or failed to accomplish. This keeps them from seeing their own performance objectively and ultimately makes things more difficult. Many leaders think working hard is the same thing as doing the hard work of leadership. It isn't. Keeping yourself busy by toiling away at drudgery is hard and wears on you over time. But that's very different from tackling the real hard work of leadership.

Do you have a tendency to mistake effort with results?

4. Feeling Like the Victim   Leaders make it harder for themselves when they feel and act like victims. I once had a phone call with a leader I was working with that really bothered me. This woman spent 30 minutes complaining about her company and her role. The more she went on, the more frustrated I became.

It's never fun to get an earful of someone else's negativity, but this call really stuck with me. I was still thinking about it later that afternoon. Eventually I realized why: This woman was a senior leader in her company, but she didn't show up as a leader. Her complaining made her sound like an employee.

Everybody gets frustrated at work. That's normal. But leaders need to be able to move through the frustration. I'll cut an employee who's complaining some slack, because he probably can't change his day-to-day circumstances that much. But a leader can.

I called this leader back and had a frank talk with her. I told her that although I understood the reasons for her frustration, she needed to step up and move forward. She needed to stop believing she was the victim and get busy tackling the hard things in her leadership role. If there's a problem, don't whine about it—fix it!

Do you show up as a victim at times? How does this set you back?

5. Being Insecure   When you are insecure as a leader, you will come off as wishy-washy, unwilling to take a stand on any issue. Maybe you don't have the courage or stomach to be a leader, and you take the easy way out on important decisions. If you're really insecure, you don't trust others and you end up micromanaging. You never let go of anything. You keep doing work you shouldn't be doing, and others around you don't grow. You may also hire weak talent for fear that stronger people will surpass you.

Other insecure leaders need to be liked by everyone. So they are agreeable—too agreeable. They never tackle the hard stuff for fear that they won't be liked. Being a leader isn't about winning a popularity contest. In fact you will learn that being liked as a leader is often overrated. You will going to be obligated to do some things that won't make everyone happy. You can't let insecurity stop you from doing what needs to be done.

Do you have insecurities that undermine your effectiveness as a leader?

6. Needing Good News   Many leaders want to hear only good news. They make their own lives harder because everyone who works with them spins information, and they never hear the real truth. If you avoid bad news, you keep yourself in a state of delusion, never confronting what's really going on. It's like being at a carnival and going to the House of Mirrors. Everything you look at is distorted. This distorted view keeps you disconnected from what's going on. You run the risk of missing things. Problems get worse, and your work gets more difficult.

Avoiding or ignoring bad news keeps you stuck. Let me put it another way: Your job as a leader is not to avoid, ignore, or deny bad news; it's to find out the bad news as early as you can so you can act before the problem becomes more complicated.

Do you want to hear only good news as a leader? Do you appreciate the impact that this is having on your team and your business?

7. Winning at All Costs Competition is a great motivator, but some leaders take it to an absurd extreme. They see everyone as an adversary or an enemy—even within their own organizations. Everything is a win-lose proposition. That extends to relationships, too; they eliminate anyone who doesn't support what they're trying to accomplish. If you're overly competitive, you won't tolerate dissenters or differing points of view. You'll most likely come across as pompous, conceited, and totally absorbed in your own personal agenda.

Excessive competition creates poor working relationships with team members and keeps you from engaging stakeholders in a genuine manner. If you can't bring people along with you, you'll make your life much harder. In today's world, you need to be a savvy influencer and collaborator. You can't just intimidate people into going along with you. You need to be able to create win–win outcomes, instead of trying to win at all costs for selfish reasons.

As a leader are you always driven to win at all costs? Do you appreciate how this strategy may be making things harder for you as a leader?

8. Waiting for Permission Some leaders don't tackle the hard work of leadership because they believe they need permission to act. I've seen leaders who constantly seem apprehensive because they are waiting for permission to lead. This is a huge source of frustration for senior-level leaders. I've often heard chief executive officers exclaim, "What are they waiting for?" Many leaders mistakenly assume they can't act without approval from senior leaders. You need to understand that you have been put in a leadership role to act and tackle the hard work of leading. You haven't been given a leadership role to be a bystander.

Social psychologists have discovered a behavioral pattern called the *bystander effect*. People don't offer to help a victim in an emergency situation if other people are present. In fact, the more people present, the less likely it is that someone in need will get help. The mere presence of other bystanders diffuses the responsibility to act.

Is this happening to you? Are you waiting around for permission or acting like a bystander?

9. Being Driven to Distraction A lot of leaders struggle with the multiple and, at times, conflicting priorities they have to address. But I find some leaders make it harder for themselves because they don't have the discipline to focus on any one thing long enough to get it done. You may be one of these leaders if you are continually distracted—always going from one issue to another, from one Band-Aid solution to the next.

When you take this approach, you never really advance. You wear yourself down. You give your employees so many conflicting instructions that they disengage. The hard things become harder and, worse, you make the easy things hard.

One senior leader I worked with spoke very openly at a forum for the company's top 100 leaders about how in the past she was prone to distraction. She explained that as she took on more senior roles, not only did she run into more problems, but they got bigger and more complicated. Initially she tried to tackle all the hard tasks. And in doing so, she became distracted.

She said she eventually realized this approach was holding her back and eroding her effectiveness as a leader. She began to work on her ability to look at her day-to-day role and cut through all the noise to figure out what was truly important for her to address. She stopped trying to tackle every problem and started to take the time to pause and reflect on the truly difficult things she needed to deal with.

In what ways might you be driven to distraction as a leader? How might you be making things harder for yourself?

10. Losing Perspective Leaders need to learn from the past, but if a single issue keeps coming up again and again, it will prevent you from leading in the future. You will make things harder for yourself and others. During a recent leadership development program, I watched three senior public sector leaders have a heated discussion. I could tell they were talking about a pretty serious issue, so I let them get into it.

But after a while, something started to bug me about the conversation. I called a time-out and said, "I've been following along pretty well, but now I'm getting confused. When did this issue happen?" In unison, they said, "Ten years ago." And here I thought they were talking about a current issue that they needed to work out. "We've spent twenty-five minutes talking about this," I said. "Can anyone tell me how this is relevant to your leadership roles today?" Silence. I continued, "I don't get how you can still be this emotionally invested in something that happened so long ago. It's clear you have all lost perspective as leaders."

Unfortunately, I've been delivering that speech a lot recently. It's all too easy for people in an organization to get into the habit of rehashing old issues. But holding on to the past doesn't help. It acts as an anchor holding you back. You have to let it go.

Sure, leaders need to learn from the past, but if you're repeatedly discussing the same old events, you have lost perspective.

Do you find yourself getting stuck because you often lose perspective? Do you appreciate the impact this loss is having on your team and how it weakens you as a leader?

Tackle the Hard Work of Leadership, and You Become Strong

The hard rule of leadership also says that if you tackle the hard work of leadership, you become strong. Moreover, it's not just you who becomes strong; it's also your team, your division, and your entire organization. Why? Because you don't get stuck. You keep things moving forward, progressing all the time, instead of letting the same issues and problems continue to dominate your life.

There are three things you need to understand to make this rule truly work in your role as a leader:

1. You need to shift how you view the hard work of leadership.
2. You need to develop a mind-set of resilience.
3. You need to build a strong sense of personal resolve.

Shift Your View

Our leadership development programs include an activity called the Future Environment Map. During the activity, participants identify key trends in their emerging business environment. They identify a host of trends in technology, the regulatory environment, customer dynamics, their competitors, and so on. We capture the ideas on large sheets of sticky notes and put them on a massive poster. As leaders look at the hundreds of ideas, they immediately grasp the complexity of their operating environment. They also start to appreciate how driving growth will be a challenge. Finally, they start to internalize the challenges they will face as leaders.

I then ask the leaders one final question: "As you look at this emerging environment, do you feel like this is the best time to be a leader in your company or the worst time?" It's an important and provocative question. Many leaders look at their emerging operating environment negatively—all they see is the hard work ahead. For them, it's the worst time to be a leader, and many question whether they are up for it.

Other leaders are more optimistic. They see opportunity. They acknowledge the complexity, the risks, and the hard work, but they react with excitement.

Stephen Covey once said, "How you see the problem is the problem." You need to start looking at the hard work of leadership in a different way. Instead of looking at it as something to avoid, start looking at it as a sign of progress. You need to be able to look at your role and your emerging environment and see all the hard work ahead of you with a sense of optimism, not pessimism.

When you shift your view in this way, you start to anticipate problems. You become more active in seeking problems out earlier, before they can impede your success. You want to hear bad news as early as you can get it, so you are in a better position to mitigate risk, tackle, and solve an issue before it gets out of control or bigger than it needs to be.

So how do you sort through all the numerous challenges and figure out what hard work you must tackle? Ask yourself: Are the results that I am accountable to deliver at risk? If your sense is that they are, then you better start addressing the issue. Then ask yourself: Is the way the work is being done inconsistent with my organization's values? This can create other issues that will require your attention. If you don't deal with the challenge head on. Finally, consider your stakeholders: Could the issue jeopardize obligation to my key stakeholders? If you sense that it might, then you need to get involved and resolve the issue.

We all need to recognize that it's our job to tackle the hard work of leadership. Stop avoiding it. You are the only one who can do it. Many of your direct reports can't, so don't wait for them—get tough.

Build Resilience

I recently met with a client to discuss his company's leadership development needs. This company was undergoing a transformational change, and its leaders were under tremendous pressure. My client explained that a key focus for development was to help the company's leaders be more resilient.

Given the challenges and pressures that leaders face, it's easy to see why resilience is so important.[1] Organizations need leaders who can recover quickly from setbacks and difficulties. They need leaders who can handle changes in their work environments and manage not only their own personal reactions to stress but also their direct reports' reactions.

However, I'm afraid that traditional views of resilience may be outdated today. The old view sees resilience like those inflatable Bozo the Clown punching bag toys, the ones you can punch and punch and they just keep bouncing back up for more. I believe many leaders think this is what resilience is about: You keep taking the punches, and you bounce back up for more. However, this approach isn't sustainable. You'll eventually wear yourself down.

Instead, you need to think about resilience in terms of how to maintain your optimal level of performance while tackling the hard work of leadership. You demonstrate true resilience when you are able to maintain optimal levels of performance by:

- Being able to hold your own in tough situations.
- Managing your thoughts, emotions, and behaviors when under pressure.
- Keeping a clear focus and a sense of optimism in stressful situations.
- Remaining confident despite hardships and difficulties.

You also demonstrate resilience when you're able to recover from challenging events. This means you are able to:

- Get yourself back on your feet after significant setbacks and disappointments.
- Transform or reframe your experience in ways that move you forward rather than keep you stuck.

- Overcome the setback and focus by identifying and learning lessons for the future.

You need to be aware of your own level of resilience in the face of obstacles, because how you respond affects the way you lead—and the people you lead. For example, when you confront a difficult situation, do you tend to see the negative or the positive first? Do you tend to minimize or catastrophize what is happening to you? Do you tend to internalize the situation (put it all on yourself) or externalize it (look everywhere but yourself)?

You can imagine how a group will respond when its leader always sees the negative first, has a tendency to catastrophize events, or loses it in the face of adversity. Your response will make the hard things even more difficult.

Resilience begins with a balanced perspective. Responding in an extreme way can undermine your effectiveness. Strive to maintain a healthy viewpoint on events while you weigh the pros and cons and seek a positive way forward. The good news is that resilience is not a trait. It's a muscle that can be exercised and strengthened. The more you tackle the hard work of leadership, the stronger you become and the more your resilience increases.

Develop Personal Resolve

Resilience is your ability to bounce back. Resolve is your ability to dig deep and push forward in the face of adversity. It comes from having a strong sense of inner purpose, drive, and tenacity that helps you rise above the pressures of leadership. It means you are able to succeed despite any obstacles, even failure.

Resolve is about perseverance and fortitude. It's about knowing deep down inside what it is you have to do and having the commitment to make it happen. It's not just about getting up when you are knocked down or when you stumble. It's that personal grit that enables you to push forward even when the odds are against you.

You call on your resolve to tackle the hard work of leadership. You use it to help you do the hard things you know are right when easier options present themselves. Resolve enables you to have that tough conversation today instead of putting it off until tomorrow or walk out of a frustrating meeting and not be distracted for the rest of the day. It's not letting whatever has happened to you define you. Learn from it and move on!

Leaders with sound resolve can find strength in the midst of a challenging situation. They find a way to generate positive energy from adversity and convert it into forward momentum. Leaders with resolve also glean lessons from their experiences that in turn help them more effectively deal with future pressures. Essentially, they stay strong because they tackle the hard parts of leadership. That's what being tough is really about.

Resolve is about taking energy from adversity. Having a good reset button—one that enables you to reframe, refocus, and move on—helps a lot.

The next time something happens during your day that tests your resolve, observe how you respond. Do you let the event disrupt your entire day? Do you take it for what it is, learn from it, and move on to the next thing? It's helpful in these moments to:

1. *Calm yourself.* Take a deep breath and get in touch with your reactions to the situation. Don't act immediately.
2. *Reframe the situation.* What's the hidden opportunity that has now emerged? In what ways can you creatively turn the situation around?
3. *Learn from it.* Ask yourself what can you learn from the situation? How might you approach it differently next time?
4. *Inspire yourself.* Based on what you have learned, leverage the energy to propel you forward. Use the lessons as inspiration.

Personal resolve is also made stronger when you can effectively manage your personal energy. Finding small consistent pockets of time or rituals, as Tony Schwartz calls them in his work at the Energy Project,[2] that are devoted to renewing your energy, can have a long-lasting effect on your ability to lead with the hard work of leadership. Sustaining your personal energy leads to an emotional and intellectual steadiness. It keeps you mentally sharp and physically strong so that you can effectively deal with the stress and pressure of today's leadership roles.

Your resolve is also strengthened when you can build a strong support network. Your resolve gets weakened if you feel isolated and disconnected as a leader. Building a healthy network inside and outside our organization is invaluable during stressful times and is a key determinant of one's overall health. You must also not cut yourself off nor become inaccessible to these relationships. Strong relationships are needed with family, relatives, and friends. They also are needed with peers and colleagues. In his great book *Who's Got Your Back*, Keith Ferrazzi writes that it's critical for us to create an inner circle of what he calls lifeline relationships, those relationships with a few trusted individuals who we can count on to offer encouragement, tough feedback when needed, and generous mutual support and to build resolve.

Finally, taking time to retreat and reflect on your leadership role from time to time will help you deal with the hard work of leadership. Make a commitment to block off uninterrupted time to pause, take a breather, and reflect on your role. I find that these moments of reflection are always valuable in helping me reconnect with the purpose of my role, the value I need to bring, and the renewed sense of energy and resolve I need to have to keep tackling the hard work.

Final Thoughts—It's Time to Get Tough

I began this chapter by saying that leadership involves hard work, and based on my discussions with leaders, it seems that things are going to get even harder. By now it should be clear to you that if you wimp out and avoid the hard work of leadership, you will weaken yourself and your organization. You will start a deadly spiral that will make you weaker and weaker. Instead, you need to build a sense of resilience and personal resolve that will help you do the hard work of leadership. Only then will you find that you are stronger and more able to tackle future challenges. It's time to get tough.

Reflect—Leadership Is Hard Work

As you reflect on the ideas in this chapter, think about your answers to the following questions:

1. What is the hard work of leadership that you must tackle in your role?
2. What hard work are you avoiding? Why are you avoiding it?
3. In what ways might you make the hard work harder for yourself? Review the 10 ways presented in this chapter and reflect on the ones that describe you.
4. What is your mind-set regarding the hard work of leadership? Do you see it all in a positive way or negative way?
5. How might you be able to strengthen your resilience?
6. In what ways do you need to strengthen your personal resolve?

CHAPTER 7

Leadership Is a Community— Connect

More and more of the leaders whom I work with today are expressing a yearning for something different in their experience of leadership. I can understand why. For most of us the experience has been mediocre.

Think of your own experience. There's a good chance you and your fellow leaders haven't been on the same page and have worked at cross-purposes because strategic clarity has been low. Or maybe the primary focus is on protecting turf and competing internally, silo against silo. Conflict seems to run rampant. Frustration is high, and getting anything done feels next to impossible.

Or your experience may be one of sheer apathy, where there is little energy or vitality. You and your fellow leaders seem to only be going through the motions, bystanders cloaked with fancy leadership titles. It's exhausting and at times demoralizing.

Whatever the experience, you may end up questioning why you ever became a leader in the first place. You also know deep down that there has to be a better way.

There is.

What if instead, you worked with a group of leaders in which everyone was truly aligned to the vision and strategy of your organization? What if there was a real sense of collaboration that enabled innovation to flourish? What if all the leaders in your organization showed up every day fully committed to being the best leaders they could possibly be? What if leaders supported one another to achieve higher levels of personal and collective performance?

This is what a genuine community of leaders feels like and it's the foundation to building a strong leadership culture that will be your ultimate differentiator.

And for many, this idea may seem like some distant dream. But the truth is that it isn't a dream; it's what you need to create excellence and opportunity in your organization.

The Missed Opportunity

In fact, I believe a community of leaders is the real missed opportunity in organizations today. If there's one thing I've learned over the past 25 years in the leadership business it's simply this: *If you can create a strong community of leaders in your organization, it will become your ultimate differentiator.* As one chief executive officer client of mine put it recently, "If I can figure out how to get our top three layers of leadership truly aligned and engaged to our strategy—fully committed to be the best leaders possible—it will be our secret sauce, our edge in the market." He is not alone in this thinking. More and more senior leaders I work with are starting to understand the power of building a strong community of leaders. That's what the final term of the leadership contract is all about and what we will focus on in this chapter.

As I explained in Chapter 2, the challenge we have is that our old models of leadership have always been about individuals—the one single hero at the top of the organization. This model may have been sufficient in a simpler time. It is becoming clear, however, that this model alone won't work in a more complex world. No one leader can have all the answers today. And when you think about it, it's actually risky to put all your faith in one individual.

For this reason, everyone is looking really closely at Apple. We all wanted to know: *How will the company fare now that Steve Jobs is no longer leading the way?*

We Are Wired for Community

If the old model of leadership has always been about individuals, then the model of the future is about a community of leaders. The good news is we are ready for it, because as humans we're wired for community.

Seth Godin, in his book *Tribes*, says that for millions of years, humans have been part of one tribe or another—a community. We can't seem to help it. Our need to belong is one of the most powerful survival mechanisms that we have. Whether it is through the small villages in which we live or the clubs and groups that we form, there seems to be an internal need for us to connect and interact with others.

Neuroscience validates this theory and shows us that feeling connected is intrinsically rewarding for each of us at the cellular level.[1] Health research also shows that the social support that comes from being part of strong communities is actually good for our health.[2] We don't need to look further than the proliferation of social media sites. Online communities have the same effect on us, tapping into our need to belong and to be connected.

If we extend this thinking to leadership, I believe the individuals who are able to build and sustain a strong community of leaders will thrive in the future. But this is a new idea, and we need to acknowledge that most of us don't live in strong communities of leaders at all. Because we've had such a focus on individual leaders, we've never truly taken the time to understand how to leverage leadership more broadly in organizations. Sure, some companies invest a lot in leadership development, but in the end, it's all being driven by a model of producing individual leaders. Very little focus is on helping to build collective leadership. Few organizations are able to truly create and sustain a strong leadership culture. As a result, the kinds of leadership culture that exist in most organizations today aren't that effective, and in some cases, they are downright dysfunctional. Let's look at a few examples.

A Rotting of Zombies

In this organization, leaders show up every day merely going through the motions. They are zombies—the walking dead. The leadership culture they create lacks vitality, focus, and positive energy. The atmosphere feels dull and mundane. Leaders don't have clarity about what they are there to do, and there is little commitment to doing the work. It can be a pretty dreadful place to be. This is what existed in the organization I joined 25 years ago.

This environment is typical in many heavily bureaucratic organizations. Performance is not strong, and trying to get anything done is next to impossible. At the individual level, it can feel stifling. You can smell the stale air of mediocrity. It's like living at the Department of Motor Vehicles when they've locked the doors, and you have no way out.

You know you are part of a rotting of zombies when your day-to-day environment lacks a real sense of urgency. There's no unifying force that brings your leaders together. There is no clear set of expectations for leaders about how they should behave and act.

In the end, leaders go through the motions. There is no sense of connection to one another or to a greater compelling vision. Rather, members are connected by their collective misery. There is apathy and learned helplessness. They are like crabs in a bucket. If one tries to escape, the others will grab him and pull him back down, thereby always preserving the same sorry state of affairs. Real leaders who try to change things for the better ultimately give up because of the huge amount of inertia. My colleague Zinta tried to change this kind of organization 25 years ago. She faced resistance at every turn. As we know, she may have also paid the price with her life—the stress of working in a leadership culture that was a rotting of zombies eventually and sadly took its toll.

I was asked to deliver the closing keynote speech on the leadership contract for a Conference Board event a while back. At the end of that talk, I challenged the audience to build a community of leaders in their workplace by reaching out and strengthening one relationship with a fellow leader—a very small step. At the end of my presentation a few folks remained behind to chat further and ask questions. One woman approached and said, "You know, Vince, I thought hard about your challenge to us, and I can't think of a colleague whom I care enough about to strengthen the relationship." She could sense my disappointment. She then proceeded to describe her day-to-day environment. She didn't know it, but she was describing a rotting of zombies, and it was wearing her down. The leadership culture was weak. There was no emotional connection among the leaders in that organization. I asked if she gained any insights from my presentation. She said, "It's clear that I have a choice to make: either to leave this place or start building community nonetheless." I don't know what she decided to do, but my hope is that she didn't just go back to being a zombie.

A League of Heroes

Many organizations have leadership cultures that can be described as a league of heroes that is often rooted in the charismatic personality of one leader—usually the founder or CEO. It's ultimately based on the old model of leadership that glorifies a hero. At times this organization can have some positive aspects if the glorified leader at the top is a person of integrity. When the glorified leader is highly narcissistic, however, the work environment goes bad fast and can become dysfunctional.

The real risk with a league of heroes is that too much rests on one individual leader. When that leader leaves, nothing sustainable is left behind. The organization dies.

I worked with an organization led by one of these glorified leaders. Greg was the founder and CEO of his company. He was a terrific individual who was extremely charismatic and very good at what he did. He was also adored by his employees. And when I say adored, I mean truly adored. It wasn't uncommon for employees located at offices around the world to have Greg's photo framed at their workstations. How many of you as leaders can say that your employees have your photo on their desks? That's the level of connection that this organization's employees had toward Greg. His impact on the company was significant. However, there was little room for other leaders to exert influence on the organization. The leadership culture was not as strong as it needed to be. Too much was on Greg because other leaders didn't step up.

Unfortunately, Greg died in a tragic accident. The company was distraught and became lost without him. Performance plummeted. A huge hole was left, and the other leaders who were thrust into senior leadership roles struggled. It took some time for the organization to get back on track and it did so only after a lot of pain. Eventually the company was sold to a competitor. It was the only way to carry on the legacy that Greg started when he created the company.

This story shows the risk taken when a leadership culture is anchored to one leader who is the hero. When it's all rooted on one leader (even if the person is great), it can turn a company upside down when the leader leaves, because nothing sustainable beyond that leader's work has been created.

A Stable of Thoroughbreds

Take a moment and picture in your mind horses at a track getting ready to race. They're in their starting gates, pawing the ground, snorting, full of restrained energy. The starting bell rings, and the horses are off, each determined to reach the finish line first.

Many organizations have leadership cultures that can be described as a stable of thoroughbreds. Leaders behave like those horses. Each is in his or her own starting gate, representing his or her department or function. They all have blinders on and are completely focused on their own objectives and priorities. As the starting bell rings, the gates open and they are off, each trying to win and cross the finish line first. The competition is fierce; it's all internally focused and highly dysfunctional.

I worked with the top 80 leaders of an organization during a leader forum event. The purpose of the meeting was to tackle many of the dysfunctional ways in which the top leaders were working with one another. A hot issue surfaced on day 2 of the program, and all hell broke loose. I let it go for a while to see if anyone would notice. Sometimes you have to do that to make leaders aware of the dysfunction they have created. After several minutes, the CEO finally did notice. She turned to me with complete frustration and exasperation and said to me, "Why can't we operate as one company?" He saw the light and understood the extent of the problems she was facing. The company's leadership culture was not sustainable. She would not be able to change the company until the leadership culture was changed.

I let the discussion continue even further until I began to notice the frustration peak among the leaders. I then stood on a table and yelled out to get their attention. "Ladies and gentleman, what's going on here?" I asked. "Let me remind you that the competition isn't in here; it's out there [I pointed to the windows], and they are beating you because you choose to spend your days fighting with one another in here."

Silence filled the room. Slowly people started to speak up, reflecting on what had happened in the room and how it was exactly like their day-to-day experiences. We continued an important discussion that slowly started to lead this group of leaders to a place of heightened awareness. The fact was that they needed to change, or they would be out of business. That imperative allowed them to refocus around what they needed to do to survive.

I have found this idea of building a "one-company" mind-set to be a big opportunity for organizations. More and more CEOs desperately want it to take hold because they know it's what will drive long-term success. However, making it a reality isn't easy, especially when you work with thoroughbreds every day.

You know your leadership culture is like a stable of thoroughbreds when senior leaders behave as heads of their functional areas rather than as true leaders of the whole organization. One or two functional areas will typically dominate the organization, and those leaders end up competing with each other, trying to be the one who is really running the company. You will typically see classic departmental structures and silos that are deeply entrenched, preventing any real collaboration, innovation, or drive.

I find the real challenge with a stable of thoroughbreds is that internal competition becomes the ultimate driving force. That's what leaders get obsessed about, consumed by, and get rewarded for. Politics, posturing, and game playing rule the day. You win when the other guy or gal loses—even when it means the other guy or gal is a colleague. You'll never build a one-company mindset in this leadership culture.

A client I worked with had two strong executives: one led marketing and the other who led research and development (R&D). Those in marketing saw themselves as the leaders of the company because they were the owners of the sales strategy. The people in R&D saw themselves as the leaders because they developed new products for customers. Both senior vice presidents were very capable, but they had created a false competition between the two parts of the organization. The internal competition was wasting considerable energy and derailing the overall success of the company.

Sometimes we artificially create this type of internal competition, whether it be sales versus marketing, head office versus the field, corporate versus lines of business. Whenever this kind of internal competition exists, in the long term it works against a company. It keeps leaders internally focused. Worse, it keeps them focused only on their own success, rather than on the collective success of the entire organization. And you see it play out in many obvious and subtle ways: departments that don't share resources, succession planning efforts that get stalled because leaders don't share talent across the organization, or lines of business that are unable to drive innovation and change in an aggressive manner.

At the extreme, getting anything done in this type of organization is absolutely painful. Everything feels like a fight and a vision of building a one-company identity is naïve at best.

It's Time to Build a Community of Leaders

Now is the time to become deliberate and build a genuine community of leaders. That's what the fourth term of the leadership contract demands from you.

Having a community of leaders means recognizing that leadership is not about individual leaders but rather the entire cadre of leaders. And when you get it right, it can be your ultimate differentiator—your truly sustainable source of competitive advantage—and it all begins with you. You can decide to start creating a community of leaders where you live every day as a leader. You don't have to be a CEO to get started.

You also don't need any special knowledge or insight. You already know what a strong community of leaders is like. One question I always ask leaders is, *What kind of climate would you need to be at your best and make your fullest contribution as a leader?*

It's remarkable to me how consistent the answer is when I ask this question. Leaders don't describe a rotting of zombies. They don't describe a league of heroes. They don't describe a stable of thoroughbreds. They rarely say, "I will be at my best in a climate of apathy, low trust, or low alignment." They always say the same thing: "I will be at my best in a climate where leaders have real clarity about the value they must bring. There's a deep commitment to the organization and to being the best possible leaders. There's high trust and mutual support among leaders and this extends into relationships with employees. Everyone is part of one company, fully committed to drive its success."

After years of asking the question over and over again and getting the same answer from leaders in all sectors, at all levels and in different countries, it seems to me we already know what we need to do. We're hardwired for it. Yet we struggle to create real leadership communities, remaining trapped instead within ineffective and even dysfunctional leadership cultures. It's time we bring about what we already intuitively know we need.

A Strong Community of Leaders—Clarity and Commitment

Every strong community of leaders that I've experienced or witnessed shares two critical characteristics: a high degree of clarity and a high degree of commitment.

First, all leaders are clear in their understanding that the community of leaders is built upon a shared aspiration for great leadership. Everyone understands that leadership will be the ultimate differentiator. A client of mine is the CEO of a financial services company, and he believes that every employee deserves a great leader. He's completely focused on making it happen. This simple idea sets the tone for the rest of the organization.

The community is not created merely to establish a better way for leaders to work together, although that does happen. Instead, the goal is to make your company more successful and drive sustainable business achievement. It's about that one-company mindset I described earlier. The community of leaders is also based on the reality that no one leader will have all the answers. Leadership is more distributed today,[3] and we must leverage the capability, ingenuity, and commitment of all leaders and employees.

Second, there is a high degree of clarity about the kind of leadership required for success. As a leader you have a clear understanding of the leadership expectations. As a leader you know what you must do to make the organization successful and the way in which you need to lead. You don't settle for lame or bad leadership. In fact, a strong community of leaders exits those individuals who consistently fail to live up to their leadership expectations and obligations. These organizations know that a few bad leaders can undermine the overall leadership culture. So they don't tolerate lame or bad leadership. Neither should you.

You will also find that there is a high degree of commitment demonstrated by leaders, first to the idea of a community of leaders and also to the work that needs to happen to make it so. You demonstrate your commitment by setting the pace and committing to being the best possible leader you can be. This is part of your decision and obligation as a leader, and it's part of your role in fulfilling the first two terms of the leadership contract. Be the leader everyone else wants to emulate.

You and your fellow leaders also demonstrate your commitment by doing the hard work of leadership. No one is a bystander or spectator. Everyone participates fully. You have the courage to call out bad leadership behavior. You challenge the community if leaders are not living up to the aspiration of great leadership. At first this will be difficult, but once you create your community of leaders, everyone will come to expect it. They will look to you for feedback, and you will look to them for feedback. You will have a deep sense of personal commitment to your fellow leaders. You will support their growth and development.

In fact, if *you* aren't living up to the level of leadership that has been set, you can count on someone in the community of leaders to reach out to you and say, "Hey, you aren't doing your job. We need you to be better. So step up!" No one is afraid to challenge another person. You will also know that everyone will have your back. You know they will be there for you to support you even when you are vulnerable.

For this community to work, you will need to show your commitment over the long term. A strong community of leaders isn't a destination to arrive at. Rather, you simply require constant work. You need to continually create ways to connect with your fellow leaders, to build and strengthen relationships, to drive even more clarity and commitment. The good news today is that social media tools can help you build that sense of connection and community among your leaders. Companies are leveraging social media to help their businesses connect with customers and other stakeholders. Ultimately social media tools are about creating connections and exchanging ideas. They will help you to enable your leaders to connect with one another and build a sense of clarity and commitment.

You will know when you've got it right because it will be a visceral feeling. You will feel the high level of clarity and commitment. You will be blown away by the level of trust and mutual support. You will feel part of something great, something special, and something rare.

If you've never experienced a strong community of leaders, at first you may not trust it, because you won't believe it's going to work. But give it time. It will be hard work, and yet it will be extremely rewarding. As a leader you'll feel liberated because you'll have a sense of confidence knowing that others have your back and are acting in your best interests and in the best interests of the organization.

I experienced this visceral feeling back in August 2011. It was days after Hurricane Irene hit the Caribbean, the U.S. East Coast, and parts of Eastern Canada, and I was flying home to Toronto after a business trip. My seat on the plane placed me in the middle of a group of eight young men. They were talking loudly, joking around, and full of excitement and energy.

I chatted with them as we took off. The most talkative member of the group, Daryl, reminded me a bit of the lead singer in a band, brimming with charisma and effortlessly able to connect with people. He introduced the rest of the group to me and explained they were a line crew for a contract utility company. They were headed to Toronto to pick up some trucks and then drive to Connecticut to repair electrical lines damaged by the hurricane.

This big mission explained why they were so excited, but as the flight continued I noticed something else about this group. They were constantly teasing one another. They shifted easily from talking about their personal lives to talking about the job they were going to do in Connecticut. It was obvious that they shared a deep connection. They weren't just friendly coworkers; they had a true bond.

I said to the group, "You guys seem really tight. Why is that?" As soon as I asked the question, I could see Daryl's demeanour change. He became still and thoughtful. He said, "Doing the kind of work we do, we're taking our lives into our hands every single day. We're like a band of brothers. We have to have each others' backs—one mistake and you can lose somebody forever."

That's what it feels like when you share a deep connection with your colleagues. That's what is possible when you are part of a strong community of leaders. But I don't think it should take a hurricane to build that powerful sense of connection and trust. Your life doesn't have to be on the line. Rather, it simply requires a common aspiration, clarity, and commitment on the part of all the leaders in your organization.

As you read this section, you might be saying to yourself, "Vince, this is all sounding pretty idealistic, soft, and fuzzy. Isn't it?" Here's the surprise: It's actually really difficult to do. We sometimes use the soft excuse to avoid doing the really difficult things needed to build a strong community of leaders.

But imagine the difference to your employees, your customers, and your shareholders. Imagine the collaboration, innovation, and productivity that result from having that community in place. It will be staggering.

Has Everyone Noticed the Change in the Room?

Rob was the CEO of a large utility company. He had been in his role for about 18 months. During that time, he had rebuilt his executive team. Even though he had a strong team, he knew they alone couldn't lead the company. He needed all his leaders aligned and on board, so he established the first leadership forum meeting for his top 200 leaders. It was a one-day event to bring the top leaders together to learn about the strategy of the company.

As he entered the meeting room that day, he was stunned by how quiet everything was. As he was getting his cup of coffee, he saw that 200 leaders were all sitting alone quietly. Very little discussion was happening. He led the day, but it was a painful experience. The leaders just sat there, listening, but not engaged in other ways. Rob said, "It was like pulling teeth."

When Rob discussed the day with his executive team, they all realized that they had a lot of strong technical leaders who were very inwardly focused. The team also realized that these leaders would not be equipped to deal with a more complex operating environment requiring them to be more nimble, competitive, and customer-centered in the face of deregulation. The experience of the leader forum confirmed Rob and the team had work to do to strengthen their group of leaders.

A leadership development program was created with the goal of starting to build a community of leaders in the organization. At first, the program met with considerable resistance. In the past, other leadership programs were seen as a large waste of time.

However, as the cohorts began to go through the program, they began to realize its value and then perceptions began to change. About a year after running a series of the intensive leadership programs, Rob held another leadership forum event for the top 200 leaders. This time when he entered the meeting room, Rob was struck by a very different vibe. As he went to get himself a cup of coffee, he noticed that this time there was a positive energy in the room that didn't exist a year before. He could see leaders talking and laughing with one another. He could tangibly feel that something profound had changed. He began his opening remarks by saying, "Good morning, everyone. Have you noticed the change in the room today?" He began to explain what he observed, what he felt, and how it differed from a year ago.

The leaders in the room agreed, and an impromptu open discussion took place. It became clear that things didn't change just in the meeting room; things changed on the job, too. Leaders talked about how they felt more optimism, more clarity, a greater receptivity to change, and a deep sense of trust and support.

One leader, Brian, shared a story to validate everyone's observations. He said he had taken part in the leadership program back in the spring and during the program built some strong relationships with a few leaders whom he hadn't really known before.

A few months after attending the program, Brian had a major crisis at work—one that he had never dealt with before. A lineman in his area died on the job. Brian had to manage the entire situation. He had to inform his people and the family of the employee. He had to manage his own grief and that of his team. Brian shared with the group that in the past he would have just tried to figure it out on his own and that there was a good chance he would have stumbled. This time he immediately reached out to his colleagues from the program and explained, "I was completely taken aback when the four of them immediately came back to me. Within a half an hour, two of them were in my office and the other two on a conference call line. And after a 20-minute discussion, they helped me figure out how to effectively handle the crisis, which I did." Brian concluded by thanking his colleagues and saying that he has never felt that kind of support before in any organization he worked for.

That's what a true community of leaders is all about. It's important to note that you don't need to be a CEO to create one. As I said earlier, that's the beauty of communities: anyone can start them. Just look to social media. There are thousands of vibrant online communities that all began with one person who got it going and gathered a following. It's the same idea in starting a community of leaders. Any leader at any level can do it. You don't have to be the CEO or a senior executive. You can start wherever you are—by staying in your department or by bringing a few leaders at your own level together. As you share the idea of a community of leaders, you will find many like-minded individuals—those like you, who yearn for a different and much more positive experience of leadership. So don't wait. Start today.

Final Thoughts—How Is Help Defined in Your Organization?

During my graduate degree program, I took a course on organizational development. My professor, Dave, was in his 70s. He was a wise and mild-mannered individual. In one class we were talking about organizational culture. I asked Dave what was the one key question he would ask in an organization to quickly gauge its culture. He said, "All you need to ask is, How is asking for help viewed in this organization?" It was a brilliant response.

Dave explained that if you are in an organization where asking for help is seen as a weakness, you can already predict many aspects of the culture. People work hard to prove themselves. Issues are never truly addressed. A sense of internal competition emerges. No one dares to be vulnerable. It's a stable of thoroughbreds.

I've used this question hundreds of times over the years, and the responses I get are always quite telling.

I have found that being able to ask for help and being confident in getting a positive response is a core characteristic of a strong community of leaders. In these leadership cultures, leaders ask for help. There is no reservation, no hesitation, no concern with proving yourself or having to look good. In a strong community of leaders, asking for help is expected for very practical reasons. Everyone understands that there is a lot of work that needs to get done and the organization can't be slowed down. When you don't ask for help, you keep your organization stuck. Issues and problems are allowed to fester, distract you, and suck the energy from your organization.

Ask yourself: How is asking for help viewed in my organization?

Reflect—Leadership Is a Community

As you reflect on the ideas in this chapter, think about your answers to the following questions:

1. As a leader, have you worked in an organization with a leadership culture that was a rotting of zombies?
2. Have you been in a league of heroes?
3. When have you been part of a stable of thoroughbreds?
4. Have you experienced a genuine community of leaders?
5. How can you build a community of leaders within your organization?

CHAPTER 8

Signing the Leadership Contract

By now you know about my leadership contract and its four terms for redefining how you lead. It begins with holding yourself to a higher standard as a leader. You commit to setting the pace for others as you strive to be the best leader you can be. First you define who you are as a leader, not solely by your technical expertise. Refusing to settle for mediocrity and no longer tolerating lame leadership in yourself and those around you are key steps.

Up to this point in time, you might have been a leader who just clicked Agree without truly understanding what you've signed. Maybe you let the lure of a new title, status, more money, and potential perks cloud your judgment. Maybe you were swept away by the opportunity and ended up underestimating what it takes to be effective. Whatever the situation, if you clicked Agree without truly understanding the four terms of the leadership contract, you can't be as effective as you need to be.

By now you also know that *leadership is a decision you have to consciously make.* You first understand there are times when you have to pause, take a time-out, and make a Big D leadership decision. You recognize that in the daily act of leading, you will also make many small d leadership decisions. Both types of decisions will shape who you are as a leader. You'll notice a visceral difference when you make these decisions more deliberately. You'll feel it, and so will those around you.

Second, you know that *leadership is an obligation and you need to step up.* You understand that it's not all about you—it's about your customers, your employees, your organization, and the communities in which you do business.

Third, you know that *leadership is hard work and you need to get tough.* You recognize that there is a lot of hard work that you as a leader must do. It's *your* work—no one else will do it, and if you don't tackle it, you will make yourself and your organization weaker.

Finally, you know that *leadership is a community and you need to connect*. No matter where you are in your organization, no matter what level of leadership role you have, you must work to build a strong community of leaders—one where there is a deep sense of alignment, mutual support, respect, and trust. You know if you can get this right, the community of leaders will set your organization apart. It will be your ultimate differentiator.

So that's the fine print of what it means to be a great leader. All that remains is for you to sign the leadership contract.

It's Time to Sign the Leadership Contract

In the blockbuster movie *The Hobbit*, Bilbo Baggins is enjoying the simple life. Then he's approached by a group of dwarves who inform him that they are on a quest to reclaim their lost kingdom and secure a treasure.

Before they start out, the dwarves present Bilbo with a contract to sign, describing his role and the contribution he'll need to make as a burglar. It looks pretty straightforward at first: out-of-pocket expenses, time required for the task, remuneration. It explains Bilbo will get one-fourteenth of any total profit, which sounds reasonable. Then one of the dwarves mentions terms regarding funeral arrangements. And Bilbo reads that they aren't liable for any lacerations, eviscerations, or incinerations sustained during the journey. By now, this contract is making the nature of the upcoming journey seem pretty clear. Thinking about the possible risks, Bilbo actually faints.

Despite his original enthusiasm, Bilbo doesn't sign the contract right away. But if he didn't sign it eventually, there would be no journey. All that talk about reclaiming a lost kingdom and treasure would be moot. It's only after he signs the contract that the journey begins. This journey will involve great challenges and even hardships, but in the end, Bilbo and the dwarves succeed in their quest.

Right now, you might be feeling a little like Bilbo, reading over all that fine print about evisceration. Up to this point in the book, we have been reviewing what the leadership contract is, what the four terms mean, and how you must put them into action. You can see how the four terms will make you a better leader. You might be inspired and motivated to put them into action. You may have probably also considered the implication of the four terms for your own leadership role. But the reality is that until you commit and sign the leadership contract, this is all moot.

Remember, the leadership contract isn't a legal document. I once did a one-day leadership forum with the top 150 leaders of an organization, and the agenda went out ahead of time with the title of my presentation ("The Leadership Contract") and a brief description. The leaders all came to the event anxious, expecting they would actually have to sign a legal contract. Once they understood what the leadership contract is really about, they settled down a bit. But in retrospect, I don't think their self-imposed anxiety was such a bad thing. It made those leaders pause and really think about this thing called leadership and whether in fact they were prepared to sign the leadership contract.

In the end, the leadership contract is an agreement you make with yourself—it's a personal and even moral obligation you alone decide to take on. I will never know whether you've actually signed it. People you work with won't know unless you tell them. But in another sense, we will all know, based on how we see you show up each and every day as a leader. If you are only going through the motions as a leader, there's a good chance you haven't signed. If you have signed, everyone will sense your commitment to being the best leader you can be. This won't make you the perfect leader—there is no perfect person—but it will definitely make you one that others want to emulate.

Once you sign the leadership contract, everything changes. You will find there is no going back. Your organization expects a lot from you, whether you are an emerging leader, a frontline manager, a mid-level manager, or an executive or C-suite leader.

Your organization needs you to step up. You need to be as strong a leader as possible so that you can make your organization strong. Your employees, customers, stakeholders, and communities are all counting on you. And when you sign the leadership contract, you make a promise to be the best leader you can possibly be.

It's a lot like when a couple decides to get married. After all the preparations and plans, it all comes down to the moment when they hear these words: "I now pronounce you husband and wife." As soon the officiant says those words, they truly become a married couple. Everything changes, but the two individuals don't change. They are the same people. But something fundamental has taken place. What has changed may not be apparent immediately, but over time it becomes obvious, as the couple continues to live together and learn what it truly means to be married and fulfill the terms of that relationship.

The same is true with the leadership contract. I won't know whether you actually ever signed it, but I will know as soon as I see you in action as a leader that you have made the personal commitment to be the best leader possible.

So it is up to *you* now—are you ready to sign the leadership contract?

The One Thing You *Cannot* Do

Before you answer, I must be clear with you on one important point: *You cannot stay in your role without signing the leadership contract.* If you do, you'll end up leading in a mediocre way. You will do a disservice to your organization and the people you lead. You will also do a disservice to yourself. So let me repeat: *You can't stay unless you sign.*

Right now, I'd like you to take a moment and reflect on the four terms of the leadership contract. Consider all the ideas we've explored together in this book so far. Review the questions that I had you reflect on at the end of each chapter. Now read the leadership contract that follows and carefully consider the words and the implications to you.

The Leadership Contract

I understand that the leadership contract represents a deep and personal commitment to being the best leader that I can be—the leader my organization needs me to be. By signing the leadership contract, I am making a personal commitment to myself. In turn, I will no longer settle for mediocrity. I will not simply go through the motions as a leader. I will be an accountable leader. I understand that I can choose to share my commitment with others, or I can keep it to myself. Either way, those around me will know that I've signed up for the leadership contract based on the way I show up each and every day as a leader.

1. Leadership Is a Decision—Make It

I understand that leadership is a decision, and by signing below, I decide to be a leader. This means that I will be aware of when I need to make Big D leadership decisions. I will also bring this clarity to my role each and every day as I make effective small d leadership decisions.

2. Leadership Is an Obligation—Step Up

I understand that I am obligated to be the best leader I can be. I have an obligation to my customers, my employees, my organization, and the communities in which we do business. I will lead in an ethical manner. I will live up to the position of responsibility that my organization has given me.

3. Leadership Is Hard Work—Get Tough

I understand that as a leader there is hard work that I must do to make my organization successful. I also understand that if I avoid the hard work, I will make myself, my team, and my organization weaker. I commit to not being a bystander or a

(continued)

(*continued*)

spectator. Instead, I will demonstrate resilience and personal resolve to tackle the hard work.

4. Leadership Is a Community—Connect

I will work to create a strong community of leaders in my organization. I will aspire to great leadership in myself and encourage it in others. I will set the tone for other leaders. I will strive to be the leader that others want to emulate. I will build relationships based on trust, respect, and mutual support. I will work to drive greater clarity and commitment among our leaders so that we can effectively execute our strategy and help make our organization successful.

■ ■ ■

I agree to the four terms of the leadership contract set out above and will demonstrate my commitment by signing below.

....

(Your Name_____) Date_____

Signing the Document

By signing the leadership contract, you are making a leadership decision. You are committing to becoming the best leader you can be for your organization and those you lead. You are consciously saying you will step up to your obligations as a leader. You will commit to tackling the hard work of leadership. You will also build a strong community of leaders within your organization. If you can agree with these terms and have the conviction to be the best leader you can, sign and date the contract.

Really, I mean it. Sign on the dotted line.

So what just happened? Did you sign? Did you do it half-heartedly or with real conviction? Did you put the book down because you thought it was a silly exercise? Remember that whatever happened, I'll never know. The important thing is that you know, and that's what being a real leader is about. The commitment you make to yourself is your first obligation as a leader.

There are a few scenarios worth addressing at this point in the process.

You Realize You Don't Want To Lead

Maybe you were about to sign and then you pulled back. Maybe you realized something about yourself: *I don't really want to be a leader.* Maybe you never have.

Congratulations. This is an important insight. Please note, there is nothing to feel bad about. It's better to be honest with yourself one way or another. As my team and I have shared the idea of the leadership contract with clients, we have encountered people in leadership roles who end up realizing they shouldn't be leading. It's something they never wanted to do, and it's something they shouldn't do. In many cases, they ended up taking on other roles in their organizations, where they continued to add value and everything worked out fine. However, some of those reluctant leaders decided to leave their organizations. That's good news, too, because those people are finally pursuing what they truly want to do in their lives. These are definitely *not* easy decisions. But you do need to be honest with yourself and your organization!

You Want to Sign, but You Don't Feel Ready

Maybe you found that you couldn't sign the leadership contract because you don't feel ready to take on a leadership role and fulfill its terms. You may have other priorities in your life that are more important, like a young family who needs your attention. That is perfectly fine. What's important is that you are making a deliberate decision not to lead—and that is actually an important leadership decision. Keep adding value as an individual contributor or by sharing your specific expertise, and when you feel ready, reread this book and then sign up.

You Have Confirmed a Decision You Already Made

Some leaders I work with say that signing the leadership contract is a confirmation of a decision they have already made in the past, just not so explicitly. You might be one of these leaders. You have fully committed to being the best leader you can be, but you've done it unconsciously. In my experience, once you consciously commit to signing and putting the leadership contract into action, it immediately takes you to another level as a leader. Your commitment grows stronger. You feel even more conviction about being a great leader than ever before.

Create Your Own Leadership Contract

Some leaders I know are so passionate about becoming great leaders that they are motivated to create their own personal leadership contract. If you are one of these leaders, then I applaud you. Take the leadership contract presented earlier in this chapter and modify it for your own needs.

If you go through all the effort to create your own contract, I strongly encourage you to go public with it. Share it with your team. You'll be amazed at the impact it will have on them and the way they will see you. But it's important not to share it with a sense of arrogance. You'll come off as pompous and pretentious. Instead let your genuine commitment come through, coupled with a sense of humility. This is a powerful combination.

Final Thoughts—Signing the Leadership Contract

This book is based on the idea that many of us have signed up for leadership roles without understanding what it truly means to be a leader. When we take on a leadership role, we know we're signing up for something important but most of us aren't fully clear what's involved. Like all those online contracts, you've clicked Agree without ever reading the terms and conditions. You show up every day trying your best, but you're never 100 percent sure you are doing what you need to do as a leader.

The leadership contract gives you the clarity you need to do what is expected of you as a leader. As you review it, it creates in you a sense of personal commitment to be the best leader you can possibly be. You will find that this experience will change you as an individual. You will feel it. It's visceral. As I said earlier in this book, not only will you feel it, but so will those around you. You might get approached by a colleague who stops you in the hallway and asks: "Hey did you lose weight? Did do something with your hair? There's something about you that's different."

That difference is simply the fact that you have now signed the leadership contract and have made the commitment to be the best leader you can be and make your organization as successful as it can be.

Reflect—Signing the Leadership Contract

As you reflect on the ideas in this chapter, think about your answers to the following questions:

1. How do you feel now that you have or have not signed the leadership contract?
2. Has anything changed in how you view yourself?
3. How will you behave differently as a leader?

CHAPTER 9

The Turning Points of Leadership

At this point, I'm assuming you've signed the leadership contract. If so, congratulations. I applaud you, and you need to give yourself a small pat on the back, too.

You might be thinking to yourself, "Now what?" It's a really good question, and the topic of this chapter. We are going to explore the implications of the leadership contract for you as a leader, whether you are an emerging leader, frontline leader, midlevel leader, or an executive. They're not that much different than those you agree when signing any other kind of contract. The act of signing is one step. The next is enacting the terms of the leadership contract in your own leadership role. Let's get to work.

If you are new to your leadership role or have been in it for a while, the ideas in this chapter will give you the clarity you need to make sure you are living up to the demands and expectations of your position.[1] Armed with these insights, you'll be able to make better personal leadership decisions and improve how you manage your leadership career and how you lead yourself during challenging times.

To help you get a clear sense of what the leadership contract will mean to you, we will return to the leadership turning points that I first introduced in Chapter 4.

Revisiting the Turning Points of Leadership

There is a quote that I've always liked from the Spanish philosopher José Ortega y Gasset. He said, "Tell me what you pay attention to, and I'll tell you who you are." If you extend this idea to leadership, it simply means that you can tell a lot about leaders based on what they pay attention to. In fact, the four terms of the leadership contract help you pay attention to the fine print of great leadership. In the process you become more deliberate as a leader because you have both the clarity and the commitment you need to become a great leader.

As you will recall from Chapter 4, a turning point is an event that causes a significant change to occur. For us as leaders there are four critical turning points where we need to pay special attention, pause, and reflect on our leadership role. The reason this is important is that the stepping-stones we traditionally relied on are now gone. Every leadership role you take on today and in the future will involve making a significant leap and not all leaders are successful at it. Studies have consistently shown that leaders, whether they are managers, mid-level leaders, or executives is high. Many fail within 18 to 24 months of starting a new role.

These leaders never intended to fail. They were like you: bright, ambitious, and fully committed to success. But it seems those qualities aren't enough to guarantee success for leaders today. As a result, you need to pause, be clear on what you are taking on, and ensure you are doing everything you can to succeed in your leadership role. This is where the four terms of the leadership contract becomes very valuable.

They provide a useful way to help you reflect on your role and give you clarity on what you specifically need to pay attention to each turning point. In turn, this positions you for success and helps you avoid the failure path that plagues so many leaders.

Turning Point 1: Emerging Leaders

The first time you even consider being a leader is a critical moment. As I described in my own personal leadership story in Chapter 1, when Zinta said to me, "You need to be in management," that was the first time anyone expressed those words to me. What surprised me was how something immediately changed in me. Those words forced me to see myself differently. And that's what happens when you are tapped on your shoulder and told you are being seen as an emerging leader.

All of a sudden you start a personal discovery process of understanding what leadership is and what that will mean to you.

Take the experience of Tariq. He was a leader in a transportation company, specializing in distribution and warehousing. He was taking part in our Knightsbridge LeaderReady program for emerging leaders. He told us that after attending the program he gained a whole new appreciation for how he would need to behave as a leader. Moving forward he quickly realized he couldn't be seen as a complainer or whiner any longer. He had to evolve from being an employee to becoming a leader. He realized that he had to set the bar higher for himself. It would no longer be appropriate for him to behave as one of the gang on the construction crew.

This insight troubled Tariq because he had already started to feel the separation building between him and those he worked with as peers. This common challenge faces all emerging leaders. The good news for Tariq was that he was open to understanding the realities of his future role, and the four terms of the leadership contract helped him.

What you will find is that when you are an emerging leader, it's often your organization that makes the first leadership decision. Someone in the company will see you as a potential leader and mostly likely will let you know it. This recognition becomes an invitation for you to start learning about what leadership is really about and whether you are suited for it.

Don't fall into the trap that many emerging leaders do: don't refuse the invitation because you think leadership will just be about more work. Yes, there is a lot of extra work and effort required when you are a leader. But there is also greater opportunity to affect your organization and your team. So your real decision at this point is to remain open and learn as much as you can about what being a leader is going to be like. It's also important that you be honest with yourself. If you don't feel you are up to being a leader, then wait until you are ready.

It's also a good time to start paying attention to your core obligation as a leader at this level: getting yourself ready to be a leader. This readiness starts with shifting your mind-set from thinking like an employee and individual contributor to thinking like a leader. Start looking for ways to show up and demonstrate your ability to lead.

A lot of the hard work that you must do as an emerging leader will be personal. Once you get the label of emerging leader, it's hard not to let it go to your head. However, if you do, everyone will know it, and it will affect your relationships with your colleagues. So it's important to remain humble.

It's also important that you start building your personal resilience and resolve by deliberately stretching yourself beyond your comfort zone. And it's a great time to pay attention to all the core people skills that you will need to excel at. Develop your ability to manage conflict, give feedback, and hold people accountable. Let me tell you from personal experience and the experience of hundreds of leaders I've worked with that it's best to learn these skills now because if you don't, your personal gaps in these areas will come back to haunt you later.

As an emerging leader you can also start paying attention to building a sense of community with fellow leaders. The critical way you can do this is by connecting with other emerging leaders in your organization. You may also find it helpful to build a small group outside your organization, either through a professional network or your own contacts. That's what I did when I was an emerging leader in my first job. I struggled to find like-minded individuals inside my organization, so I gathered a few colleagues and friends and set up a network myself. We would get together about four to six times a year to talk about leadership and our careers. I personally found it was a valuable experience because it helped me cope with the challenges I was facing within my own organization.

Start looking for ways to bring forward your ideas and start showing up as a leader, even if you don't have the title or the role yet. You need to start building your resilience to be able to deal with the increased demands and adversity that will come from having your first leadership role. Take advantage of whatever development opportunities your organization may offer. Look for ways to expand your skills on the job through special assignments and projects. Also begin to observe other leaders in action. See what works for them and what might get in their way. Over time you will start to gain clarity on how you will want to show up as a leader.

Finally, I hope that you never lose sight of this reality: *Your organization is going to need a constant supply of strong leaders for the future.* If you decide to be one, the future is yours for the taking. But you must first decide to get clear about what it means to be a leader and have the commitment to make it happen. Your key action at this turning point is to be honest with yourself.

Turning Point 2: Frontline Leaders

If you are a frontline leader, you have one of the most critical leadership roles in your organization. I know you may not believe it, but it's true. You are the closest person to the employees and customers of your organization. You have the proverbial finger on the pulse of what is happening. You can have considerable impact. You will start noticing that you are held to a different standard. Excuses that may be tolerated for employees will no longer be acceptable for you. You will realize soon enough that leadership isn't about excuses—it's now all about accountability for results.

The first time you decide to become a supervisor or manager of people is one of the most important leadership decisions you will ever make. You realize you are no longer an individual contributor. It's no longer about you. You have made the decision to stand apart from the pack and be the leader, someone committed to adding more value to your organization. You have suddenly entered a different zone, and it starts to affect you in ways that you never would have suspected.

Take Thomas, for example. He became the supervisor of a team that he was a member of. It changed the relationships that he had with his peers. He knew that. What he didn't realize is how much. This became clear to him when the team organized a summer outing and didn't invite him. At first he was a little hurt by it. However, when he put his leadership hat on, he understood that it was good for his team to do social things without the boss. He realized that's the price that one pays as a leader at times.

One of the things I realized when I was a frontline leader is that your team also makes a leadership decision: They decide whether they will follow you. If they do, your job will be a lot easier. If they don't, you will have some hard work ahead. So pay attention to your team. Be deliberate when making small d leadership decisions during team meetings. You'll be amazed how far deliberateness and consistency on your part will go in helping your team drive high performance.

What you will also find as a frontline leader is that you start really thinking about the responsibility and obligations you have to your organization (or at least you should be). Your core obligations are twofold: to drive the performance of your team and to learn the essentials of your new role.

You quickly realize that you are now accountable for the performance of your team. Depending on your role, your span of control can be considerable. You may be responsible for 10, 20, or more direct reports—no easy task. In fact, you really start feeling a bit of the heat as a leader because you are truly accountable the larger the group you lead is.

You will also need to master the leadership essentials that you will count on for the rest of your career—key skills such as coaching, listening, delegating, setting clear expectations and managing performance, holding people accountable, and con-fronting conflict. Like any emerging leader, it is best that you learn to master these skills now, because if you don't, your effectiveness, if and when, in a more senior leadership role later on. You will find your day will become consumed by the people issues. In fact, you'll be surprised how much time they will take and how much personal energy they will sap from you.

Although you may not find your obligation to your communities as obvious, I encourage you to find ways to give back to society. It's important that you develop the ability to pay attention to this broader obligation now, because it will become an increasing expectation as you move into more senior level roles.

Some of the hardest work you will face as a leader centers on the shift from being a doer to becoming a delegator. Many frontline leaders struggle with it. You may have a role that still demands that you do the work in addition to managing others. You will most likely also have the greatest technical expertise on the team. Your team will look to you as the expert, which can be a difficult transition for some people.

The other hard work that you will need to do is to recast from where you get your personal sense of gratification. As an individual contributor it primarily would have come from your own accomplishments and performance. Now you need to shift this source and gain personal gratification from building your team and watching everyone grow. You will need to let go of the desire for personal glory and replace it with the desire for glory for the team. You will have to let go of rating your performance based on your own contribution and instead be judged by your team's contribution.

Your final challenge at this level is to not isolate yourself. Reach out to leaders at your level in your own organization. Find ways to connect with them at work or after work outside the office. Day to day, it's also important to build the habit of connecting with your fellow leaders in real ways. Instead of always sending e-mails, pick up the phone—better yet, walk down the hall and sit with a colleague to discuss an issue. These small but important practices to connect with other leaders will be invaluable to you over your leadership career.

A few final thoughts for frontline leaders: There will be times when you feel ignored by your organization. It's nothing personal; it's just the way some organizations run. Don't let this get to you. The good news is that more and more organizations are recognizing that frontline leaders are critical to their overall success. In fact, I believe there may not be a better time to be a frontline leader than today.

Turning Point 3: Mid-Level Leaders

Mid-level and senior leadership roles are the glue within any organization. At this level it's all about your ability to have organizational impact; this skill is what you will be judged on as a leader.

As you make the leadership decision at this level, you will come face-to-face with the challenge of letting go. What drove your success up to this point—your strong technical expertise—is now being replaced with that murky world of organization-wide leadership. In this world, your success is defined and measured largely by your ability to influence, collaborate, and drive innovation. You will need to break down silos to get the work done and meet customer needs.

What I realized when I had a role at this level is that no one's leadership decision is a onetime single event. Every day you show up to work and face significant challenges and demands, and they'll force you to regularly ask yourself: *Am I up for this? Am I prepared to do what is necessary? Do I have the stomach to take this on?* And depending on your day, you may be asking these questions a lot.

These questions are critical because this is the level where you may find yourself checking out or starting to settle. When this happens, you run the risk of showing up each day and merely going through the motions as a leader. If you find yourself doing this, stop and question your leadership decision altogether.

Your core obligation at this level is to have organizational impact! This means not looking to your executives for permission or approval to do things. You must be able to effectively work across your organization with other leaders to drive change and create high performance. It will be no longer about your own team or department. For probably the first time you start realizing that your obligation is to now be an ambassador of your organization. *You are the company!* You are expected to lead inside and outside. You will start thinking much more about your obligation to the communities in which you do business. Depending on your role, you may be the face of your company to your local community.

There is a lot of hard work at this level. The people issues continue, but they will feel harder to handle because now that you are also dealing with other senior leaders, ego, politics, and insecurity become part of your everyday experiences in working with others.

The drama can be intense at times, and you will need to learn how to deal with it. You will be challenged to be strategic you're at the same time dealing—with tactical priorities. You'll be in the middle—caught between pressures from the front line and from the executive level and you'll feel like you are always reacting or in firefighting mode.

This is the world of big project implementation. You may not be a sponsor of these big projects, but you will own their successful execution. And although you will live in one department or line of business, you will also need to start having an enterprise-wide perspective.

It is at this level where your resilience and personal resolve will get truly tested. You will learn whether you are up for it. You will also start getting a glimpse of whether you have what it takes to succeed in a more senior-level role. But to do move forward, you will need to overcome some of the traps that weaken leaders at the mid-level.

One leader whom I worked with was a brilliant individual. Tazeen's personal performance was outstanding. She also had developed strong personal relationships with her team members.

Unfortunately, she blurred the line between being a leader and being a friend to and team members behaved very causally with her team. She wanted to be seen as one of the team and as a result didn't she tackle performance issues.

Some members of the team took advantage of her good nature. Although she was liked, she was seen as being a weak leader. Ultimately this stalled her career. Executives saw him as a capable middle manager, but they didn't have the confidence that he would succeed at the more senior levels of the organization. Tazeen was struggling with her role and the power that came with it.

As a senior leader, you will have more power than you did at lower levels. It's important to understand how to handle it, how to share it with others, and how not to abuse it.

All the hard work at this level is critical and necessary because it will prepare you for what's to come in a more senior leadership role. One of the changes you will experience is that you will now manage other managers, many of whom have greater expertise than you do in their own specialty areas. The hard work before you is to forge a strong team when you don't have the technical expertise. You will need to rely on the advice and judgment of others and make decisions based on their suggestions. This level of trust may be unsettling for you.

All this pressure can get to you, and at times, you might feel disconnected and isolated. Yet the irony is that it is at this level precisely when a true sense of a community of leaders can be created. The challenge you will face is that you will be living in a stable of thoroughbreds. Your day-to-day climate may be one of internal competition—silos fighting silos.

You must change that climate. You must reach out to your fellow senior leaders. Because you will be collaborating on many company-wide projects, there will be natural opportunities to connect. Take the time to build truly positive and healthy relationships with your peers, relationships that will have a positive impact on the work you are doing. Form your own support group within your organization, made up of a small number of trusted colleagues. Leverage social media tools to connect across geographies. There are more ways to connect with fellow leaders today than ever before.

It's also important that you do not insulate yourself or stay too internally focused. Stay connected with leaders in your industry outside your organization. The primary opportunity at this level is that you will be able to transform the nature of your relationships with peers and colleagues based on trust, respect, and mutual support.

I find many mid-level and senior-level leaders underestimate the impact that they can actually have on their organizations. The reality is that as organizations continue to become more lean and streamlined, leadership roles at the middle are critical. Don't lose sight of this detail. Your company's success is in your hands. As always, the decision is yours. I encourage you to make it and lead your company to greatness.

Turning Point 4: Executive Leaders

Welcome to the big leagues. You've finally made it to an executive or C-suite leadership role. Everything will feel more intense: the accountability, the scrutiny, the need for professional maturity. At the same time, becoming an executive leader is an amazing opportunity to shape the future of your organization.

The time at which you decide to take on one of these roles is also critical because your impact is very significant. Although these roles have big titles, big compensation, big perks, and so on, you need to decide why you really want the role. Are you genuinely motivated to have a positive and enduring impact on your organization? Or is it all about you—your ego and your personal needs? Are you prepared to take your leadership to a very different level by becoming a great leader, one whom your employees and stakeholders will look up to?

An important factor in making a leadership decision at this level will be your relationship with your boss: the chief executive officer (CEO) or chair of the board. This relationship will need to be strong if you will have any chance of succeeding. Make sure you take the time to truly gauge what this relationship will be like. If your sense is that it won't be strong, then you need to address this before you decide to take on the role.

Your Big D leadership decisions will demand that you be honest with yourself. Many leaders aspire to the executive ranks, but few make it and even fewer succeed. You need to have the self-awareness to know whether you are cut out for these demanding roles. You may find you are better suited to remain in a mid-level or senior leadership role. This is perfectly fine. Our organizations need strong leaders at all levels.

Your obligation as an executive leader is fairly straightforward— you must lead the future. You need to shape your environment, create a strategy that will drive sustainable growth, and establish a strong culture that will attract and keep the best talent. You should feel the weight of your obligation to your customers, employees, fellow executives, board, and shareholders. The game changes once again—you now really start to understand the many obligations you must live up to.

You should also start recognizing that as an executive, you have moral and fiduciary obligations: *You must leave the organization better than you found it*. You must scale the organization beyond yourself and create a business model that will drive sustainable growth. You must be externally focused and build strong stakeholder relationships.

Your time is no longer spent reacting—anticipating, shaping, and executing are your new priorites. What you should also realize is also no longer just about your function or line of business. You must wear the proverbial corporate hat, thinking about the success of the entire enterprise.

Another key obligation is to build a strong management team and ensure you have succession in place. In fact, many CEOs whom I've worked with believe building a strong team is one of their most critical obligations to their company. Boards judge CEOs on their ability to build strong teams. Teams at the top are vital to the success of your company[2]—not only because they are necessary to drive company performance, but also because you have an obligation to build leadership continuity and ensure succession issues are being addressed.

There is considerable hard work at this level, much of which is made more difficult because of the constant scrutiny you will face. Just consider the scrutiny and criticism that Marissa Mayer, president and CEO of Yahoo!, endured during her first year on the job. As we've explored earlier in this book, when you are under this kind of scrutiny, fear may creep into the back of your mind. You don't want to be the leader who screws it all up or brings your organization down. Your mistakes make it to the front pages of newspapers and business magazines and go viral on Twitter. Those are the risks and the challenges. You learn that you are the face of your organization, and its reputation often hinges on your own reputation. Your resilience and resolve get tested in a completely different way.

I worked with a small group of CEOs who were in transition and were clients of the Knightsbridge Executive Outplacement Program. We were talking about the ideas of the leadership contract and spent considerable time talking about the hard work at the executive level. They commented that some of the hardest work involved is making difficult business decisions such as terminating an employee or closing a failing business unit. Even if these decisions are the right ones for the company, they still carry a personal toll for leaders.

Of the four leadership turning points, it is at the executive level where you can make your impact felt in your organization by creating a true community of leaders in a way that will become the ultimate differentiator for your company. At a personal level, you can set the pace for others and model great leadership and ensure your senior team does as well.

As we discussed earlier in the book, executive roles can be isolating and at times lonely. You need to break this sense of isolation. Build a network of close relationships inside and outside your organization. I find many CEOs, for example, will have a small team of external advisors and colleagues they can go to for advice, support, and a sense of community. You don't have to be a CEO to establish this. Reach out and find leaders who are in a similar role as yours (inside or outside your organization) and connect on a regular basis. In the end, leadership is all about the connections you make.

I believe there is no better time than today to be an executive-level leader. If you can figure out how to leverage social media, you now have a platform to share your organization's story in ways that you couldn't a decade ago. If you are able to create a truly inspiring company and place to work, you will attract the best and the brightest in your industry. You also have the opportunity to have an impact on global and social levels. These opportunities are what the executive level puts before you.

Final Thoughts—The Turning Points of Leadership

As I described earlier in this book, as organizations have become leaner over the years, many critical roles no longer exist. In the past, these roles acted as stepping-stones to help you grow and mature as a leader. Today, the stepping-stones are gone, and the transition between each of the turning points can feel like a considerable leap. For this reason I believe so many leaders derail within the first one to two years in their roles. They have made the leap without truly understanding the fine print and the expectations of the leadership role. The good news is that the four terms of the leadership contract provide a practical and useful way to help you gain a clear understanding of what you are signing up for, what you have to pay attention to, and what you must do to become a great leader at each turning point.

Reflect—The Turning Points of Leadership

As you reflect on the ideas in this chapter, think about your answers to the following questions:

1. What does the leadership contract mean to you?
2. What new insight did you gain about your leadership role?
3. What specific areas must you pay attention to now as a leader?
4. What clarity did you gain about how to apply the four terms of the leadership contract to your role?
5. In what ways has this clarity affected your commitment to be the best leader you can be?

CHAPTER 10

Putting the Leadership Contract into Action

In *Into the Blast Furnace: The Forging of a CEO's Conscience*, author Courtney Pratt shares his experience as the leader of a large steel manufacturer going through a complex and drawn-out corporate restructuring.

The company was in serious financial trouble brought on by years of poor leadership and management neglect. Technology was out of date, costs were out of control, the pension deficit had ballooned, and the relationship with the union was extremely adversarial.

To make matters worse, the chief executive officer (CEO) of the company left. Given the poor state of the company, the board knew it would be impossible for them to successfully attract and secure a new CEO. So they asked Pratt if he would lead the company. Pratt was a seasoned C-suite leader. He made the leadership decision to take on the role even though he knew it was going to be an extremely challenging and difficult experience.

Soon after assuming the role, Pratt had a closer look at the financials of the company and realized the situation was far worse than anyone had ever anticipated. The company was in a desperate financial state and was going to run out of cash very soon. Pratt and his management team explored all options, and it soon became apparent that the only way forward was to enter bankruptcy protection so that they could restructure the company and position it for future growth.

Pratt was clear about his obligations during this process. He wanted to make sure the organization came out of bankruptcy protection as a stronger company, while preserving and protecting pensions—two tensions he would have to manage aggressively. At the time his plan made perfect sense. But soon after the company entered bankruptcy protection, steel prices unexpectedly began to rise, driven by significant demand from China—a country hungry for resources to fuel its dramatic growth. As the weeks went by, steel prices hit historic highs.

All of a sudden a new problem emerged for Pratt. The company started to turn a profit because of the high steel prices. His stakeholders accused him of prematurely moving the company into bankruptcy protection. However, he knew the real state of the company. He understood once steel prices returned to normal levels, the company would once again be back in the same desperate situation. Since the company was now turning a profit, there was little or no urgency on the part of Pratt's primary stakeholders to do the hard work still required to do the hard work still required to turn the company around.

Pratt faced another hurdle. In most bankruptcy protection cases, a company needs to work on having its creditors support the restructuring plan. In the case, there were three key stakeholders: the union, the government, and the creditors, each of whom could veto the restructuring plan. To further complicate the situation, many of the creditors were hedge fund managers who saw an immediate opportunity to profit from the restructuring.

Pratt and the company needed to find a way forward that would meet the needs of all three distinct stakeholders while keeping the needs and interests of employees, customers, suppliers, and shareholders front and center throughout the process. That was Pratt's objective. However, he had another higher aspiration. He also wanted to engage in the process in a way that enabled everyone to take the high road and stay out of the mud.

Throughout the process, Pratt also believed he had an obligation to keep all his primary stakeholders informed of developments during the restructuring. He committed to regular, honest, and straightforward communications. He wrote a letter to employees almost every week, held regular town hall meetings, responded to employees' questions, put out media releases almost every week, and held weekly conference calls for customers and suppliers. He also maintained a connection with the local community by appearing regularly on a local radio show.

After two years of negotiations and countless false starts, he finally got a deal approved.

As a leader, Pratt was challenged like never before. He needed to demonstrate resilience and personal resolve. He needed to be firm, yet flexible. He also needed to juggle multiple stakeholder relationships (many of whom had competing interests) and do it in a transparent manner.

Pratt said of his experience, "During our court-supervised restructuring, foremost in my mind, always, was protecting the 6,000 jobs and upward of 10,000 retiree pensions that were on the line as we fought to stabilize this debt-ridden company. Even with that clarity of purpose, this was no easy ride." It's clear from his words that leadership is hard work.

He also said that as a CEO of a large corporation you can never truly know every employee. You can never truly appreciate the thousands of people affected by your decisions as a leader. Yet, because you are the leader, you are accountable to each and every one of them and you must do your best to manage the complex forces that affect their livelihoods. Pratt continued by saying, "You are accountable to shareholders, to the banks, to the bondholders who lend the company money, to the communities where the business operates, and to the governments. You're on the hook in so many ways, and that center of a matrix of responsibility can tear you apart if you don't have an appetite for complexity."

Pratt also knew that to succeed he would need a strong community of leaders. His challenge was that he had a very disparate group that needed to become a community: executive leaders, members of the board, and other leaders and advisors. He knew that all these leaders needed to be singing from the same song sheet—they needed clarity and commitment.

He began by establishing the terms of how they would need to operate, including always taking the high road, being respectful (as much as possible), and committing to engaging in open and transparent communications with all stakeholders.

When a small number of leaders could not or would not align to these terms, he would confront the issues, and in a few cases, he had to ask them to leave the organization.

It wasn't an easy two years for Pratt and his community of leaders. It was a period of constant crisis and adversity. Yet they had resilience and developed a collective sense of personal resolve.

Pratt believed that the adversity brought them closer together as leaders. At the end of the process, all the leaders said it was the toughest two years of their working lives but that it was also the most rewarding experience they had ever had. This shows how leaders can come together in a crisis, pull through adversity, and become stronger both individually and collectively. That's what a community of leaders can be like.

This story clearly describes to me the kind of complex challenges that leaders face today and will continue to face in the future. Your challenges and pressures will undoubtly be different but still complex. What has also changed for leaders is the high level of scrutiny faced by multiple perspectives—customers, employees, shareholders, stakeholders, and market analysts. The world for leaders is a very different place than it was even just a generation ago.

This is why we need a leadership contract. As Pratt learned, you can't lead without making the conscious and deliberate decision to be a leader. The pressures will tear you apart if you don't have the clarity and commitment to truly be a leader. His story illustrates that you can't lead without the clarity of your obligations and a clear sense of commitment to yourself, your customers, your organization, your employees, and the communities in which you operate. You see the hard work ahead of you, and you realize you must get tough to succeed—you need resilience and personal resolve, as Pratt and his team did. Finally, his story shows us the power that comes from building a strong community of leaders—one that can withstand and rise above the complexity and pressures of leadership in today's organizations.

In this final chapter, we will explore how you can put the leadership contract into action in three ways:

- Through a set of foundational strategies that will create the strong basis from which you will lead
- Through a series of daily, quarterly, and annual practices to ensure you keep living up to the four terms of the leadership contract
- Through implementation of the leadership contract within your own organization

Foundational Strategies for Putting the Leadership Contract into Action

There are three foundational strategies that you need to put in place to help you become the leader you need to be. Let's explore each in detail.

1. Create Your Own Personal Leadership Story

In the first chapter of this book I shared my personal leadership story to help you understand the experiences that have shaped me as a leader.

When I work with leaders in our development programs, I ask them what has most influenced their leadership; they all say that experience was the best teacher. But experiences can only be the best teacher if we take time to reflect on them and consider how they have shaped us. What you will find is that you've had many experiences, some positive and some negative, that forge who you are as a leader and how you act every single day.

The problem is that if you are like most leaders, you aren't really aware of how these experiences have shaped you. When you don't have this clarity, you don't have the necessary foundation to put the leadership contract into action.

Start building this foundation by understanding your own personal leadership story. In the following sections I outline the steps for you. In addition, go to www.thecommunityofleaders.com and download a free workbook that will guide you step-by-step through the process we use with thousands of leaders in our development programs.

Determine Your Critical Leadership Experiences Pause now for a moment and think about the critical experiences that you believe have really shaped you to be the leader you are today. I bet stories are already coming to mind. Some may be of peak experiences where you had a significant impact as a leader—where you were at your best. Other stories are more negative, moments in which you struggled, worked for the worst boss on the planet, faced adversity, or had your personal resolve tested.

Identify Common Themes and Patterns Once you've determined the critical leadership experiences, look at them as a whole and identify any common patterns and themes. What were you most proud of? How did you handle adversity? What insights do you glean about your personal resilience and resolve? What we generally find with this activity is that you immediately come away with a sense of clarity regarding who you are as a leader and why you lead in the way you do. This level of clarity enables you to be much more effective in making good leadership decisions.

Share Your Leadership Story One of the most powerful things you can do as a leader is share your story with those you work with. I have been surprised by the impact it has on others. Often these stories enable your direct reports to better understand who you are as a leader, what's important to you, and in turn what influences how you lead.

2. Define Your Value as a Leader

As I have described in this chapter, once you decide to lead, you quickly learn you are going to be held to a higher standard.

You have obligations that go beyond you. You have obligations to your customers, employees, shareholders, and communities.

To fulfill your obligations, you need to be clear on the value you must deliver as a leader. Take a moment to think about those to whom you are obligated and ask yourself: How would they define the value I have to bring as a leader? Better yet, go ask them. Talk to your customers, employees, peers across your organization, and stakeholders in your community that are dependent on you and your organization. They will have an answer. You will learn whether you are seen as a leader with credibility. You just need to ask.

Here is a set of questions that I use with my direct reports, customers, and internal and external stakeholders to help me determine my value as a leader:

1. What is the primary leadership value that this individual provides to the organization?
2. What are this individual's current strengths as a leader?
3. Where are this individual's key development opportunities?
4. What blind spots does this individual need to pay attention to?
5. How effectively is this individual living up to the four terms of the leadership contract?
6. Identify one action that this leader must do to increase his or her value as a leader.

3. Sign the Leadership Contract at Each Turning Point

As I already noted, the four leadership turning points are critical moments in your career as a leader, and at each one, you must pause and reflect on what you are signing up for. Once you are offered a leadership role at a turning point, you need to understand that your world will change as a leader. Each one of these moments represents a Big D leadership opportunity. You need to pause and get clarity by asking yourself:

- What's the role really about?
- What are the expectations?

- What will success look like?
- What value must I bring as a leader?
- What impact must I have?

You must also pause and reflect on your degree of commitment by asking yourself:

- Am I up for this?
- Am I fully committed to doing what I need to do to make my team and company succeed?
- Am I prepared for the hardships that will come my way?
- Am I committing for the right reasons, or am I doing this only to feed my ego?

Once you are satisfied with your answers to these questions, re-sign the leadership contract to solidify your commitment with yourself.

Regular Practices to Put the Leadership Contract into Action

By this stage, as you begin to put the four terms into action, I'm sure it's become clear to you that these terms don't exist in isolation from one another. They are interdependent. They evolve every single day as you lead. In other words, you don't put them into effect only once; you put them to action on a daily, quarterly, and annual basis.

Daily Actions

A client of mine, Priya, is the senior vice president of human resources for a large financial services organization. After she read my first e-book summarizing the ideas of the leadership contract, she sent me an e-mail telling me how much she loved the ideas. She said she immediately saw how she could put the four terms into action on a daily basis. She even said she intended to ask herself the following four questions every single morning before she started work:

1. What leadership decision do I have to make today? Is there a Big D or small d leadership decision that I will face?
2. What leadership obligation do I have to live up to today?
3. What hard work do I have to tackle today as a leader?
4. Which relationship with a colleague do I need to make stronger today in order to continue to build a community of leaders?

Imagine the focus that answering these questions brings to Priya's approach to leadership. She positions herself to live the four terms as she leads.

Other leaders have shared with me that they also use the four questions when they are dealing with a business or leadership dilemma and no clear answer is apparent. Imagine that something unexpectedly comes up during the day, something that's a real challenge for you: an issue with an employee, a serious conflict with a customer or supplier, or something that's gone awry with a stakeholder.

All eyes are on you. You have to resolve the issue. How do you make sure you respond in the best possible way? Ask yourself the four questions presented in this chapter, and the way forward will be perfectly clear. You'll immediately know what you have to do as a leader. I know this because I've done it many times in my own role, and it works. These questions force you to think about your dilemmas more objectively. You'll keep your leadership obligations in sight. You'll end up doing the right thing as a leader.

Quarterly Actions

Each quarter, set aside two to three hours to reflect on your leadership. How did you do over the prior three months? What were some of the critical leadership decisions (Big D and small d) that you made? What value did you bring to those you are obligated to? What hard work did you tackle? What hard work did you avoid? Over these months, did you become stronger as a leader or weaker? How did you strengthen the sense of community among the leaders in your organization? Looking ahead to the next quarter, how will you continue to put the four terms of the leadership contract into action? If you are working with a leadership coach, discuss these questions with her or him. You may also find it helpful to work with a trusted colleague who is part of your community of leaders.

Annual Actions

You should also take dedicated time on an annual basis, again maybe two or three hours, to reflect on the questions in this chapter. Think of this task as your own personal leadership retreat. It's also a good time to solicit feedback from others, too.

Here's what I do every year. In December, my leadership team and I send out an anonymous survey to members of our team, colleagues across Knightsbridge, and select customers and other stakeholders. The survey includes the six questions I shared earlier that help determine your leadership value.

Once all the responses are back, I go through them to identify key themes and summarize the data. My team members do the same. Then we meet to review our results, clarify the themes, gain more insight, and personally commit to improve how we are leading and how we are supporting one another. I've worked on many multirater and 360 projects with clients, and I find this set of six straightforward questions to be one of the best ways to get feedback on yourself as a leader. The feedback is always candid, direct, and meaningful.

Determine the timing that works best for you. I do mine in December because that's the mid-point of our fiscal year. This way I can get feedback on how I've done in the first half of the year and figure out what I need to focus on for the rest of the year. This way I keep my feedback focused on the business. You may find it helpful to align your annual leadership checkup with your organization's performance review process. In the end, the important thing is to make a yearly commitment to review the four terms of the leadership contract and evaluate how you are putting them into action.

This process also gives you a chance to renew your commitment, like a married couple renewing their wedding vows. In addition, you may find it valuable for you to renew your personal commitment to the leadership contract by re-signing it annually.

Putting the Leadership Contract into Action within Your Organization

I'm often asked, "Can I put the leadership contract into action within my own organization?" Well, as I've already suggested, the answer is *yes!* In fact, I believe it's a key obligation of senior- and executive-level leaders to do precisely this! If you can get that high degree of clarity and commitment from all your leaders, it will transform your organization. It will immediately take your company to another level of effectiveness and high performance. It will become your ultimate differentiator.

Revisiting the Iron Ring Ceremony

In Chapter 5, I described the ritual called the Iron Ring Ceremony that the engineering profession uses to help newly graduated engineers understand their obligations to society. The Iron Ring is placed on the little finger of the working hand as a symbol and daily reminder of the obligations to public safety that come with being an engineer. As I described, a new iron ring has many rough edges to symbolize that a young engineer is rough and inexperienced. This instills a sense of humility in the young engineer and a recognition that he or she still has a lot to learn. Because the ring is worn on the working hand, the rough edges begin to smooth out as the engineer gains experience—and hopefully wisdom. The ring is given to the young engineer by a professional engineer, who is obligated to mentor the candidate.

This kind of ritual is missing in leadership today. One powerful way to put the leadership contract into action within your organization is to create an Iron Ring–style ceremony for new leaders. Let's call it the Leadership Contract Ceremony. Imagine if every time someone assumed a significant leadership role (at each of the four Big D turning points), your organization formally acknowledged it—not just by sending out an e-mail announcing the role change, but with a small event acknowledging your leaders for taking on the new roles and reminding them and others of the expectations and obligations they must fulfill. A few of my clients have started to do this as part of a way of closing off an emerging leaders program or a frontline leadership development program. It's a formal and public way to acknowledge that these leaders have committed to and signed the leadership contract.

The Community of Leaders Manifesto

Another way to put the leadership contract into action in your organization is to adopt the Community of Leaders Manifesto. A manifesto is essentially a written and public declaration of a group's intentions that clarifies their collective aspirations. The Declaration of Independence is probably one of the most important manifestos ever created.

The Community of Leaders Manifesto (which can be downloaded at www.thecommunityofleaders.com) outlines the commitment that you and your leaders must make to create a strong community of leaders in your organization. It clarifies what you and your fellow leaders need to aspire to create. As a result, it establishes a sense of unity. Finally, it's a powerful source of inspiration for you, for your fellow leaders, and for your employees. Imagine if your employees went to work each day knowing their leaders were truly committed to putting the ideas in this manifesto into practice. It would truly be a game changer—it would truly immediately transform your broader culture!

Print the manifesto and share it with your colleagues. Discuss whether you are living up to the ideas of the manifesto and how you can get stronger. If you want to connect with leaders outside your own organization to discuss these ideas, visit my website, www.thecommunityofleaders.com.

The Community of Leaders Manifesto

We are done with the old model of leadership that has glorified heroes.

We are done settling for mediocrity.

We will not be lame leaders.

We will stop going through the motions.

We will put an end to the isolation that we feel every day.

We will not be disconnected from one another.

We will not put up with a climate of apathy and low trust.

We will put an end to all the infighting and competition.

We will stop building silos.

We will stop working at cross-purposes.

Instead, we resolve to create a strong community of leaders—one where there is high clarity on what we are trying to accomplish as leaders to make our organization great.

We will share a collective aspiration and passion for great leadership.

We will set an example to other organizations.

We will build the best leaders in our industry.

We will operate as one company.

We will be aligned to our strategy.

We will drive collaboration and innovation across our organization.

(continued)

> (*continued*)
>
> We will build strong relationships with one another.
>
> We will make one another stronger, not weaker.
>
> Once we build a strong community of leaders, it will become our ultimate differentiator. It will be our true and everlasting source of competitive advantage.
>
> It all starts with each one of us. It all starts with a decision to lead in a more deliberate way—with greater personal clarity and commitment.

I encourage you to use the Community of Leaders Manifesto by bringing it to life in your own organization. You can start with a small team of fellow leaders and make a commitment to one another. You can also work to implement it more broadly across a level of leaders or your entire leadership cadre. Don't worry that other leaders may not find this change worthwhile. In my experience, people are hungry for an open and honest conversation about leadership. This manifesto gives you the language to start having those conversations in your own organization, among your own leaders.

Create Your Own Organization's Leadership Contract

Another powerful way to put the leadership contract into action is to create an unique one for your own organization. I worked with the CEO and senior vice president of strategy and talent of a health care organization. They were so excited about the idea of the leadership contract that they wanted to create their own. They felt the timing was right because the organization was going through an evolution. They were about to introduce a new strategic plan to the top 120 leaders. However, they wanted to make sure the leaders understood not only the strategy, but also their role in executing it.

Up until now, the organization hadn't done a great job of developing and supporting its leaders. It was time to change that. My team and I helped them create a custom leadership contract (see "Our Leadership Contract" on this page). We conducted interviews and focus groups to understand all the issues and then began to draft a set of terms. We validated these terms with other leaders and then designed a two-day leadership forum.

On day 1 the CEO revealed the new strategic plan. On day 2, we introduced the leadership contract and began the process of helping the leaders understand the terms so that they could sign up. The leaders had a very strong positive reaction to their own leadership contract. Many said they were both exhilarated and scared by the terms. Their organization was drawing a line in the sand about great leadership, something that leaders desperately had wanted to do but didn't know how up untill now. The leadership contract gave them a way. But they also understood the contract meant increased accountability—no more excuses or blaming. They were now going to lead as one community of leaders with clarity and commitment.

The Leadership Contract for a Health Care Organization

I, as a leader, commit to the following terms of our leadership contract.

- I will lead with courage. I will make tough decisions and have difficult conversations that are in the best interests of our organization.
- I will lead by developing myself. It will also be essential that I create engaging environments where people have meaningful opportunities to grow.

(continued)

(*continued*)

- I will lead through relationships. Successful strategy execution is ultimately a function of having these strong relationships with employees, patients, funders, and other key stakeholders.
- I will lead with the big picture in mind. I will align both business and team priorities. This enterprise-wide perspective is necessary to effectively operate across the organization to achieve shared strategic goals.
- I will lead with accountability. I will step up, tackle challenges, and bring solutions, rather than problems, to the table.

We will work together to lead as one community of leaders.

Six months after the leaders signed their contracts, I was chatting with Andy, the senior vice president of strategy and talent. He said to me, "You won't believe what this leadership contract has done for our organization. It's gone viral. Managers have taken it to their teams. Employees have embraced it. Our manufacturing facility created a huge poster, and all the employees signed it. Everyone is taking it seriously. It's clear that there was a hunger for accountability, real clarity, and real commitment on the part of leaders and employees. The amazing thing is that it just happened—the executive team didn't force it. It came from the organization."

I was surprised by what Andy said. I knew the potential power of the idea of the leadership contract and its four terms, but I didn't realize it could have such widespread impact. I really admire this organization's determination to put the leadership contract into action for all leaders. They are starting to realize what I've believed throughout my 25 years in the leadership industry: When you can get all your leaders sharing the same aspiration, the same clarity about what they are trying to do as leaders and the same deep commitment to creating a community of leaders, something powerful will happen, something that will become the ultimate competitive advantage!

Final Thoughts—Redefining How We Lead

When you internalize the four terms of the leadership contract and commit to putting them in action, you will reap the rewards:

- *You will stand out as a role model to others, because your decision to lead means you are setting the pace for everyone else as a leader.* You will be the leader others want to emulate. You will be more deliberate as a leader, leading with greater clarity and commitment.
- *You will bring greater value to your organization because you'll never lose sight of your leadership obligations.* You'll be clear on what you need to do for your customers, employees, stakeholders, and the communities in which you do business. You'll also be clear about your obligation to be the best leader you can be. You'll know there's no settling for mediocrity.
- *You will continually move your organization forward because you won't shy away from the hard work of leadership.* You will have the courage, resilience, and resolve to take on the hard work because you'll know if you don't, no one else will. As a result you'll find more collaboration, more innovation, and a higher level of sustained performance.
- *Finally, you'll realize it's not all about you or any one individual leader.* You'll commit to building a community of leaders wherever you happen to be in your organization, regardless of your role or level. You will provide opportunities for others to grow as leaders. You will realize the greatest gift a leader can give is the opportunity for another to lead. You'll help leaders connect with

one another to build a climate of high trust and mutual support. You will create a strong leadership culture. And when you get this step right, this community of leaders will be the ultimate differentiator for your organization.

In the end, when you put the leadership contract into action, you will redefine how you lead. You will begin to be the leader your organization truly needs you to be.

Imagine if all the leaders in your organization made the same commitment. You would be leading your company to greatness.

Now imagine if every leader in every organization did the same. We wouldn't just redefine leadership—we would change the way the world works!

NOTES

Introduction

1. http://www-935.ibm.com/services/us/ceo/ceostudy2010/index.html.
2. Studies consistently show that the vast majority of us routinely click Agree or Accept buttons without reading the terms and conditions of online contracts: http://www.guardian.co.uk/money/2011/may/11/terms-conditions-small-print-big-problems.

Chapter 1: My Personal Leadership Story

1. The term *K-Factor* was coined by one of our Executive Search partners, Lisa Knight.

Chapter 2: What's Wrong with Leadership Today?

1. http://management.fortune.cnn.com/2012/06/29/ceos-loneliness-isolation.
2. http://www.inc.com/maeghan-ouimet/real-cost-bad-bosses.html.
3. http://www.maritz.com/Maritz-Poll/2010/Maritz-Poll-Reveals-Employees-Lack-Trust-in-their-Workplace.aspx.

Chapter 3: Why We Need a Leadership Contract

1. http://www.foxnews.com/tech/2010/04/15/online-shoppers-unknowingly-sold-souls.

Chapter 4: Leadership Is a Decision—Make It

1. Economist Garrett Hardin illustrated this example and referred to it as the "Tragedy of the Commons." He published his ideas in *Science* 162, no. 3859 (December 13, 1968), pp. 1243–1248.

Chapter 5: Leadership Is an Obligation—Step Up

1. http://www.nytimes.com/2012/05/02/world/europe/murdoch-hacking-scandal-to-be-examined-by-british-parliamentary-panel.html?pagewanted=1&_r=2&hp&

and http://www.guardian.co.uk/media/2012/may/01/phone-hacking-report-wilful-blindness.

2. http://www.parliament.uk/business/committees/committees-a-z/commons-select/culture-media-and-sport-committee/news/news-international-and-phone-hacking-report-publication.

3. http://www.ncbi.nlm.nih.gov/pmc/articles/PMC1142333.

4. http://blogs.hbr.org/kellerman/2008/11/leadership_malpractice.html; also, check out her website at http://barbarakellerman.com.

5. http://management.fortune.cnn.com/2011/11/18/sam-palmisano-ibm.

6. http://blogs.hbr.org/hbsfaculty/2012/01/how-ibms-sam-palmisano-redefin.html.

7. Gandz, J., M. Crossan, G. Seijts, and G. Stephenson. *Leadership on Trial.* (Ontario: Richard Ivey School of Business, 2008).

8. See Porter, M. E., and M. R. Kramer. *Creating Shared Value.* (Boston: Harvard Business Review, 2011). Available at http://hbr.org/product/creating-shared-value/an/R1101C-PDF-ENG.

9. Learn more about Conscious Capitalism at http://consciouscapitalism.org.

10. http://blogs.hbr.org/kanter/2012/11/five-self-defeating-behaviors.html.

Chapter 6: Leadership Is Hard Work—Get Tough

1. I would like to thank Dr. Kim Rogers and Dr. Alex Vincent of Knightsbridge for their contributions to the ideas on resilience in this chapter.

2. Check out the work of Tony Schwartz at http://www.theenergyproject.com.

Chapter 7: Leadership Is a Community—Connect

1. http://blogs.hbr.org/cs/2012/11/are_you_getting_personal_as_a.html.

2. The research demonstrates that those of us with high-quality and/or a large quantity of social networks have a decreased risk of mortality compared with those who have low-quality or a low quantity of social relationships. Social isolation is often identified a major risk factor for mortality. http://www.ncbi.nlm.nih.gov/pmc/articles/PMC2729718.

3. http://blogs.hbr.org/imagining-the-future-of-leadership/2010/04/its-not-all-about-me-its-all-a.html.

Chapter 9: The Turning Points of Leadership

1. I would like to thank Tammy Heermann of Knightsbridge for her contributions to the ideas in this chapter.

2. Check out the work of my Knightsbridge colleague Dr. Liane Davey at www.changeyourteam.com for insights, resources, and tools to build strong teams.

ACKNOWLEDGMENTS

Throughout my career I have had the good fortune of working with outstanding professionals—individuals who have supported me, provided me the privilege to work in their organizations, and encouraged me to develop the ideas shared in this book.

I want to thank my clients. I'm indebted to you for having the confidence in me, my team, and Knightsbridge, and for giving us the opportunity to work with your organizations.

I wish to thank David Shaw, founder and chief executive officer of Knightsbridge Human Capital Solutions. David, I appreciate your unending support and belief in 'my vision for the leadership business and the value it will bring to our company.

I want to also acknowledge my colleagues at Knightsbridge—some of the smartest, most passionate, and most creative professionals in the human capital industry. I want to especially acknowledge Dr. Ralph Shedletsky, our chief customer officer, and Victoria Davies, our chief financial officer. Your constant support and wisdom have helped me immeasurably as a leader within our firm. Thanks also to other members of the Knightsbridge executive team: Brad Beveridge, Leslie Carter, Catharine Larkin, Kelly McDougald, Frances Randle, Regan Sorensen, and Paul Tucker. I'm grateful for the opportunity to work with each of you.

Many thanks to Courtney Pratt, the chair of the Knightsbridge Human Capital Board. I value the mentoring you have provided me over the years and the example you have set as a leader.

Thank you to the board of directors of Knightsbridge Human Capital Solutions for your support.

To Lori Dyne and Mirren Hinchley, thank you for your expertise in all things social media and research.

To my fellow team members in the Knightsbridge Leadership Solutions practice, I am always in awe of what you accomplish for our clients. It is a sheer pleasure to work with each of you every single day. I also want to acknowledge the members of my leadership team, including Audra August, Bryan Benjamin, Dr. Liane Davey, Tammy Heermann, and Brian Wellman. Thank you for your drive, commitment, and enthusiasm. An extra thank you to Liane. I deeply appreciate all of your support and collaboration over the past seven years. Your unbridled energy coupled with your powerful ideas makes you one of the best minds in our industry. A special acknowledgment to Razia Garda—thank you for your tireless efforts to keep me organized and productive.

Thank you also to Dr. Nick Morgan, Nikki Smith-Morgan, Sarah Morgan, and Emma Wyatt of Public Words. Your full commitment to me and my ideas are deeply valued.

A big thank you goes to the team at John Wiley & Sons, who contributed greatly to this project. A special thank you is due to Shannon Vargo, Elana Schulman, and Lauren Freestone.

Writing a book, while managing the demands of an executive role, consulting on client engagements, and leading a busy home life, could only be accomplished with the support of my family, including my parents, Cam and Maria; my mother-in-law, Carmela; my brother, Robert; my sisters-in-law, Mary and Rosanna; and my brother-in-law, John, and nephew, Nicolas.

To my children, Mateo, Tomas, and Alessia. You are the constant inspiration in my life. I am proud of the young leaders you are becoming. An extra thank you to my daughter Alessia and your inspiration for the design of the book cover.

Finally, to my wife, Elizabeth. Once again you constantly amaze me with your unending support and encouragement. Thank you for your excellent advice and ideas on the manuscript. Nothing I do is possible without you. Thank you for everything you do for our family.

ABOUT THE AUTHOR

Vince Molinaro, PhD is the Global Managing Director of the Leadership Practice within Knightsbridge Human Capital Solutions, a firm dedicated to helping organizations seamlessly execute their business strategies through their people.

He advises senior executives and boards on how to make leadership culture their ultimate business differentiator. Over his career Vince has developed award-winning leadership development programs for organizations in the energy, financial services, technology, professional services, and public sectors.

As a business leader, Vince sets the leadership bar high for himself and his team. He doesn't just preach the leadership stuff—he works hard to live it.

An engaging and thought-provoking speaker, Vince conducts keynote presentations for corporations, conferences, and management retreats.

He's conducted pioneering research into the future of leadership and shares his insights through his blogs. He's also the author of three books including *The Leadership Contract*, *Leadership Solutions*, and *The Leadership Gap*, all published by John Wiley & Sons, Inc. You can follow him on Twitter @VinceMolinaro.

ABOUT KNIGHTSBRIDGE HUMAN CAPITAL SOLUTIONS

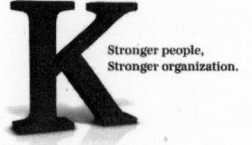 Knightsbridge is a unique human capital solutions company designed from the outset to be truly integrated—to seamlessly bring together a diverse group of experts to find, develop, and optimize your people. Our consultants bring together their diverse expertise as a unified team, to provide our clients with deeper insight into their human capital needs and deliver more strategic, customized solutions based on an integrated view.

Across North America and around the world through our global partnerships with AMROP and The Career Star Group, Knightsbridge works with clients to seamlessly execute their strategy through people.

Knightsbridge has the people you need, when you need stronger people.

www.knightsbridge.com

INDEX

Bring *The Leadership Contract* into Your Organization and Drive Real Accountability among your Leaders

The Leadership Contract Workshop

Based on the powerful ideas of Vince Molinaro's best-selling book, *The Leadership Contract: The Fine Print to Becoming a Great Leader* this hands-on workshop will transform how you lead. It will shift your mind-set of what it means to be a leader and how to step up to the real obligations of your role. You will develop skills that increase your resilience and personal resolve to tackle the hard work of leadership needed to make your organization successful.

Does Your Company Need a Leadership Contract?

If you need to drive real accountability across your organization, Knightsbridge Human Capital Solutions can help your organization create its own Leadership Contract. This will ensure your leaders are clear on what's expected of them and how they need to step up individually and collectively to drive success and execute your strategy.

Start building a strong leadership culture today. To learn more about The Leadership Contract workshop and our other leadership development programs go to www.knightsbridge.com.

Knightsbridge Leadership Development Programs for leaders at all levels

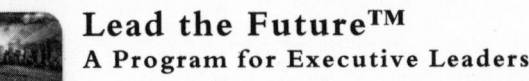

Lead the Future™
A Program for Executive Leaders

Lead the Future™ challenges executives to take a hard look at their own leadership and how it continues to evolve to meet the demands of a dynamic business environment. From that foundation, leaders strengthen their ability to anticipate, shape and execute business strategy.

Lead with Impact™
A Program for Mid- to Senior Leaders

Lead with Impact™ helps senior leaders see beyond their teams to grasp the importance of leading across the organization—to effectively lead change and execute strategy. The program focuses on the importance of influencing a broad range of stakeholders to drive collaboration and innovation. Leaders gain greater insight and clarity about their value, new skills for real collaboration, and how to align and engage their teams to higher levels of performance.

LeaderAccelerator™
A Program for High Potentials

LeaderAccelerator™ fast-tracks the careers of high potentials by equipping them with greater self-awareness, and providing experiential assignments where they can apply new skills. Through ongoing access to and feedback from peers, senior leaders, mentors, coaches, and assessors, this critical cadre of leaders gains organizational visibility, personal and business insight, and the skill and confidence required to play pivotal roles in the execution of strategy in their organizations.

LeaderEssentials™
A Program for New or Frontline Leaders

LeaderEssentials™ builds on management fundamentals to help leaders appreciate the critical role of the frontline today. The program provides tangible tools and practical application, while stretching frontline leaders to take a more strategic perspective. Participants come away with increased confidence and accountability to lead at the personal, team and organizational level.

LeaderReady™
A Program for Emerging Leaders

LeaderReady™ exposes those individuals considering taking on first time management roles to what it truly means to be a leader. The program articulates the expectations of leaders, provides simulations of critical leadership scenarios, and assists participants as they create action plans for their career development. Emerging leaders walk away with a clear sense of what is required to be a successful leader and a plan to be ready.

658.4092 Mol
Molinaro, Vince, 1962-
The leadership contract

AUG   2013